Coping with Japan

Coping with Japan

John Randle
with
Mariko Watanabe

Basil Blackwell

© John Randle and Mariko Watanabe 1985

First published 1985
Reprinted and first published in paperback 1987

Basil Blackwell Ltd
108 Cowley Road, Oxford OX4 1JF, UK

Basil Blackwell Inc.
432 Park Avenue South, Suite 1503
New York, NY 10016, USA

British Library Cataloguing in Publication Data

Randle, John
   Coping with Japan.
   1. Japan – Description and travel – 1945– – Guide-books
   I. Title
   915.2'0448   DS805.2

   ISBN 0–631–13451–4
   ISBN 0–631–15443–4 Pbk

Library of Congress Cataloging in Publication Data

Randle, John.
   Coping with Japan.
   Bibliography: p.
   Includes index.
   1. Japan – Description and travel – 1945 – Guide books.
   I. Watanabe, Mariko. II. Title
   DS805.2.R36 1985   915.2'0448   84–28283

   ISBN 0–631–13451–4
   ISBN 0–631–15443–4 (pbk.)

Typeset by Opus, Oxford
Printed in Great Britain by Billing & Sons Ltd, Worcester

Contents

Contents

Acknowledgements

We would like to thank the many people who have given help and encouragement in the preparation of this book. They include members of the Japan National Tourist Organization, especially Mr Akira Fukunaga of the London office and Mr Sammy Suzuki in Tokyo; members of the Japan External Trade Relations Organization, in particular Mr Hiro Kanda in Tokyo and Mr John Whiffen in London; Mr Malcolm Dennes of the Exports to Japan Unit, British Overseas Trade Board; Mr Fuminori Tamai, Director, the Australia-Japan Academic and Cultural Centre; staff of the American Embassy, Tokyo; Miss Minako Furuta, Mr Mike Tokunaga and Professor and Mrs Deto who made clear many difficult points in Japanese culture; Mr Tomohiko Motoyama who worked hard to provide budget advice for fellow students; and the many members of the British community in Tokyo who answered questionnaires about their experiences in coping with Japan. Professor Yoshio Maya on sabbatical leave from Nihon University was conveniently at hand in Oxford to read the drafts of this book as they appeared and to offer numerous useful comments and suggestions. Mrs Phil Guy was a patient typist. The maps and a number of the illustrations were drawn specially for this book by Mr Hiroshi Umemura in Tokyo.

J. R. and M. W.

Introduction

There has been little movement of population to or from the islands of Japan for 1,500 years. The Japanese people have developed a unique language, religion (Shinto) and culture, and have on the whole shown considerable discrimination in what they have taken from the outside world. At a critical juncture in Japan's history when western nations were beginning to colonize the Far East, she locked herself away for two and a half centuries. Arguably, it was the feudalism of that isolated period that did most to solidify Japan's national characteristics, which make Japanese society so conspicuous in the modern world. To an outsider those characteristics may seem somewhat old-fashioned: loyalty, obedience and honesty.

The rest of the world has always baffled the Japanese. They realize that by turning inwards they miss much and perhaps get dangerously out of step. But the ability to accept the new and to adapt is a vitally important part of the Japanese character. In the last century the Japanese accepted industrialization and parliamentary democracy. In this century they quietly accepted sweeping changes after the last war. The image of Japanese society as not one rock but a series of rocks that shift and change, but in the end remain rocks, has often been employed. Japan also has a very modern image – beautiful shops, gleaming office blocks and excellent highways. In fact, Japanese people visiting European cities think them very old and perhaps rather grey. But Japan's appearance should not delude the visitor into thinking that the country has westernized; rather it has become spectacularly modernized.

Visitors, whether on business or pleasure, will be given excellent treatment in Japan, travelling in ease, comfort and safety, anywhere they will. On the practical level coping with Japan presents perhaps fewer problems than most countries, but if coping with the country includes understanding the way the society works and trying to work with it, then the visitor must be prepared for perpetual studenthood.

One thing is certain: if you have the chance to go to Japan, take it. Its charm and attractions are unique. You will be left with enchanting memories.

Planning your flight
It is wise to shop around for flights. From Europe paying the regular fare on airlines would make Japan one of the most expensive places in the world to reach.

There are three main routes to Japan from Europe.

The prestige route is the polar route via Anchorage, Alaska (flying time about 17 hours).

The shortest route to Japan is via Moscow (about 14 hours flying time), and one can make a stop-over in Moscow by arrangement with the Russian tourist authorities.

The southern route, via the Middle East and southern Asia, is the longest (flying time varies from 22 to 32 hours), but it has its advantages. One can usually pick up the cheapest tickets on this route. There is also the opportunity of making stop-overs in exotic places such as Bangkok, Singapore and Hong Kong.

Both Singapore and Hong Kong have excellent duty-free shopping within the airport. (Tokyo's duty-free shops are not particularly good.)

Australians going to Japan will, of course, have the opportunity to make similar stop-overs; Singapore is a favourite spot for Australians. Americans crossing the Pacific are inclined to drop in to the state of Hawaii. For those with plenty of time it is well worth investigating 'round-the-world' tickets, which allow you to make Japan just one stop on an extensive itinerary.

Airports
Narita
The New Tokyo International Airport at Narita is the largest and handles domestic and international flights. It has had a short but eventful history, involving some of the most violent protests of the

postwar period. Security is tight. Passengers flying from the airport have to pay a passenger service facility charge of 2,000 yen.

Narita is 60 kilometres from downtown Tokyo. ('Downtown' is a well understood term.) Allow an hour and a half for travelling by car or train between the airport and Tokyo.

A taxi to downtown Tokyo is prohibitively expensive. The airport bus is called a limousine, and there are services to a number of points. One is to the Tokyo City Air Terminal (TCAT, pronounced 'Tee-Cat') and to Tokyo Station. Another service goes to major hotels and to Shinjuku Station. There are also limousines to Ikebukuro, to Tokyo's second airport, Haneda, and to the city of Yokohama. Alternatively, you can take the train called the Skyliner, which operates between Narita and Ueno Station.

Osaka

Osaka International Airport is the second largest airport in Japan. Limousines travel from there to downtown Osaka (30 minutes), Kobe (40 minutes) and Kyoto (60 minutes).

Haneda

Haneda airport is a short distance from downtown Tokyo, with which it is connected by monorail. Haneda handles only domestic flights except for the flights of China Airlines.

Other airports

Niigata, Nagoya, Fukuoka, Kumamoto, Kagoshima and Naha (Okinawa) airports handle international flights.

By land and sea

From Europe you can go to Japan on the Trans-Siberian Railway with connecting shipping links. This is not cheap, but it is something of an adventure. The number of possible stop-over sites is being increased, so that you can now see not only places in Russia, but also Peking and the Great Wall.

Baggage
Clothes to take with you

The Japanese dress very well, usually with great taste and in the latest fashion. Tourists are unlikely to offend by not being smart and should dress comfortably; businessmen should go for suits; businesswomen for suits or a formal dress.

Seasonal differences are marked in Japan, but there is also great variation between north and south and between high and low ground, so even at the height of summer you should take a sweater. In December, January and February you will need winter wear. In June, July, August and September light clothing is essential. In the other two seasons, spring and autumn, days are generally warm and evenings range from cool to cold. (See the section on climate in *Travelling around Japan*.)

You should take with you everything you will need to wear, as prices in Japan are high, and sizes may cause a problem. Pack plenty of newish socks and tights, as you will probably spend a lot of time walking about in buildings without shoes on, and your foreign feet will be on view.

Travelling light   If you are planning to travel around Japan, you will need small, 'squashy' bags, as there is nowhere to store large suitcases or valises on a train.

Customs   Travellers are allowed to take 200 cigarettes or the equivalent in pipe/cigar tobacco, three bottles of alcohol and two ounces of perfume into Japan. With the alcohol allowance you can reward deserving Japanese of your acquaintance. (Best bets are cognac or a good whisky.) Cigarettes (until recently a government monopoly in Japan) are cheaper there than, for example, in Britain.

Japanese customs officers may well confiscate anything they consider to be pornographic. All narcotic drugs, including marijuana, are strictly forbidden in Japan.

Residency   The rapidly growing foreign community in Japan reflects Japan's rise as an economic superpower. It is a very attractive country for the foreigner to live in – crime is low and the standard of living high. There is a great deal to do – explore the country, learn something of Japanese culture and learn the language. You will be very comfortable, but don't delude yourself that you will be assimilated by Japanese society – you will always be a privileged and perhaps pampered outsider.

Basic advice is to allow yourself some time to settle in to Japan – don't expect to have all the answers after six months. Make an effort to get involved and be courageous about starting new activities.

If you want to go it alone in Japan – writing, studying, etc. – speak to someone at the Japanese consulate about procedures before leaving for Japan. Look around for floating scholarships and bursaries.

As a resident in the country you will be accorded a residency status, which determines how long you can stay and what you can do while you are in Japan (see below for visas). Here are the commonest categories:

4–1–5	employed by a foreign company	up to 3 years
4–1–6(–2)	students	1 year
4–1–7	university teachers, researchers	up to 3 years
4–1–8	cultural entrants	up to 1 year
4–1–9	entertainers, athletes	up to 60 days
4–1–10	missionaries	up to 3 years
4–1–11	press, radio and TV	up to 3 years
4–1–16–1	short term residents (a catch-all category)	up to 3 years
4–1–16–3	teachers of English conversation	up to 3 years

Pay and pensions

A number of foreigners now work full time for a Japanese company and thereby receive bonuses twice a year and are included in the company pension scheme. Westerners working part-time in Japanese companies usually receive a higher hourly rate than their Japanese counterparts. (Full-timers are paid the same rates as a Japanese.)

Taxation

If a person is considered a non-permanent resident (usually living in Japan for under five years), only the income they derive from Japanese sources and income from elsewhere remitted to them in Japan is liable to Japanese income tax. However, a permanent resident's whole income world-wide is liable to income tax.

The standard income tax rate is low compared with Britain – currently starting at about 10 per cent. This is withheld by employers. If a foreigner believes he (or she) should receive a tax rebate, or if he has other income to declare, he should go to the tax office by 15 March. The tax year runs from 1 April to 31 March, but you should file tax information *in advance* – some people begin to file as early as January.

Some categories of foreign worker are exempt from income tax for a period (for example, some university professors).

Children's education Children who do not speak Japanese are most unlikely to be able to go to Japanese schools. There are a large number of private schools in Japan catering to the foreign community and to those Japanese who wish to have their children educated in English. (There are also French- and German-speaking schools.) A list of schools, including descriptions, is given in *Living in Japan*, published by the American Chamber of Commerce.

Getting there – and staying on

The best source of information for the tourist is the **Information**
Japan National Tourist Organization (JNTO), which
has offices in Australia, Britain, Canada, France, West
Germany, the USA (and other countries) and pro-
duces a series of booklets on visiting the country. In
Japan the JNTO operates three Tourist Information
Centres (TICs). These are located at:

New Tokyo International Airport, Narita (tel. 0476–
32–8711)
Kotani Building, 1–6–6 Yurakucho, Chiyoda-ku,
Tokyo (tel. 502–1461)
Kyoto Tower Building, Higashi-Shiokojicho,
Shimogyo-ku, Kyoto (tel. 075–371–5649).

(Please note that throughout the book the area codes
for phone numbers in Japan have only been included
in telephone numbers for places other than Tokyo.
To dial a Tokyo number from outside the city use the
Tokyo area code 03.)
The Teletourist Service is a free tape-recorded
telephone service run by the JNTO, which tells you
what is going on in and around Tokyo. Dial:

503–2911 for the English-language service;
503–2926 for the French-language service.

The Japan Travel-Phone is an advisory service
available for the use of foreigners who need information on travel or who are in trouble. In Tokyo or
Kyoto telephone the TIC direct. Outside those two
cities dial 106 and say to the operator slowly, in
English, 'Collect call TIC, please.' TIC offices are the
places to go for specific advice on accommodation.
TICs will not make bookings, however.

Visas
Visiting Japan as a tourist

Technically, everyone visiting Japan must have a valid visa. However, reciprocal agreements between Japan and a number of countries mean that citizens of certain countries can travel to Japan without a visa if they are on holiday, visiting companies or attending conventions or sporting events and are not planning to make money on their trip.

If you come from the UK or Ireland you can stay for up to 180 days without a visa. There are generous arrangements for most West European countries. Canadians can stay 90 days and New Zealanders 30 days without visas. Australians and Americans need visas, which are given for 60-day periods without fuss. Apply to the Japanese Embassy or Consulate in your own country in good time.

Working in Japan

A visa is required by *anyone* who is going to work in Japan or who plans to stay longer than the tourist's limit. (It is at this point that you are given a particular residency status.) A visa must be obtained before you set out. Allow plenty of time (at least two months) for formalities to be completed. (The Japanese consular authorities are efficient. However, there may be delays in your being able to furnish the necessary documentation.)

A prospective employer will generally require you to sign a contract and return it to him. He will then apply for a visa to the Ministry of Justice and the Department of Immigration on your behalf. You will ultimately be sent a certificate issued by the Ministry of Justice, which, on presentation at a Japanese Consulate, will automatically secure your visa. You will have to pay a fee at the Consulate and provide two passport-size photographs of yourself.

If you go to Japan as a tourist and decide to work there, you will have to leave Japan to obtain a work visa. This may be arranged in Hong Kong, for example. Contact the Department of Immigration before you leave Japan.

Alien registration

Every visitor must also register as an alien if their stay in Japan will exceed 90 days. Registration is just a formality. Go to the Alien Registration Office of the ward (district) or town in which you are living before the 90 days are up. Present your passport and three passport-size photographs of yourself. You will be asked to fill in a form and to be fingerprinted (this is done with charm). Children under 14 must be registered but do not need to have their fingerprints taken.

You should receive your Alien Registration Card on the spot. Carry this with you at all times. Changes in the information that you have supplied on your form must be communicated to the Office within 14 days.

If your stay in Japan is to be a lengthy one, leaving the country and returning to it within your period of residence – if you go on holiday or make a business trip, for example – you will need to visit an Immigration Office before you leave Japan and acquire a re-entry permit (issued on the spot). You can get a single or a multiple re-entry permit. If you anticipate making several trips to and from Japan in a year, it is both more economical and more convenient to acquire a multiple re-entry permit, which is valid for one year. A multiple permit costs *about* ¥6,000, a single permit ¥3,000. The multiple permit is given at the discretion of the Immigration Office. Immigration Offices are to be found at the following addresses in Tokyo and Osaka:

Re-entry permits

Central Immigration Office
    Immigration Bureau, Ministry of Justice
    1–1 Kasumigaseki 1-chome
    Chiyoda-ku
    Tokyo 100
    (tel. 580–4111)

Tokyo Immigration Service Centre
    World Import Mart Building
    6F Sunshine City
    1–3 Higashi-Ikebukuro 3-chome
    Toshima-ku
    Tokyo 170
    (tel. 986–2271)

Osaka Regional Immigration Bureau
2–31 Tani-machi
Higashi-ku
Osaka 547
(tel. 06–941–0771)

There are also offices in Sapporo, Sendai, Nagoya, Takamatsu, Hiroshima and Fukuoka.

Stop-overs Stop-overs in Japan are permitted for plane and ship passengers (72 hours) and for ship passengers (15 days), at the discretion of the Japanese Immigration Office and when arrangements have been made in advance by the airline or shipping company. However, to be safe, people from countries who need a visa to enter Japan should have a visa and not rely on this method of entering the country.

Health insurance If you are travelling from Britain, western Europe, the USA, Australia or New Zealand, you will not need any vaccinations before entering Japan. At your port of entry you may be asked to complete a form listing any recent illnesses you may have had.

Japan is very clean, and the water is good. It is a healthy place, but it is always wise to take out full health insurance cover from home.

Anyone working in Japan will almost certainly have health insurance arranged by his or her employer.

Foreign residents not covered by any other scheme may apply at their ward offices for municipally funded health insurance, which will cover 70 per cent of medical costs.

Accommodation

There is a large range of accommodation in Japan, most of it very good indeed. If you want a two-centre holiday only (usually Tokyo and Kyoto), some airlines (for example, Korean) offer good deals. But you can do your own booking when you are in Japan or in advance with the help of the JNTO or a travel agent.

Broadly, there are two types of accommodation: western and traditional. With western accommodation visitors have an individual room and sleep in a bed. With traditional accommodation you sleep on the floor on *futon* (mattresses). There may be other differences, in the kinds of food provided and the washing facilities available. Prices vary greatly in both the western and traditional sectors, and some of the best traditional 'hotels' top the Hilton in price.

Western-style accommodation

'Western' accommodation is never quite the same as it is in the West! Nice touches creep in, like freshly laundered *yukata* (loose bathrobes) being left on your bed every night, and slippers (impossibly small) waiting by the door.

Large hotels

The familiar western names have invaded Japan – the Hilton, Holiday Inn, Hyatt, etc. Japan also has its own hotel chains, such as the Prince, New Otani, Tokyu. Standards are very high indeed, and Japan has a high position in the international hotel league.

Japan in general, and Tokyo in particular, has experienced a remarkable boom in hotel construction in the last 10 years. Tokyo is a great international centre, and is perhaps the premier focus for conferences and congresses in the East. But you don't only see international businessmen in the large Japanese hotels. All sorts of Japanese make full use of them, the unlikeliest being the masses of teenagers in school uniforms, who at examination time put up in the more luxurious hotels to be near the exam halls and in the best possible mood to sit their exams.

It is very common to invite someone to a hotel for a coffee or for a drink, or choose the hotel lobby as a meeting point. Hotels often have excellent shopping facilities (including a post office) and sometimes superb gardens.

Business hotels   Business hotels are so called because they are supposed to meet the basic requirements of the businessman. Guests are provided with a room, a western bed, a TV set, a fridge for drinks, and a bathroom. Breakfasts are usually served in the dining-room. There is no room service, but there are always numerous vending machines in the corridors, offering everything from whisky to toothpaste.

The term 'business hotel' (pronounced *hoteru*) is well understood by taxi drivers and the trade, and they are good places to go for no-frills accommodation at a very reasonable price.

Frivolous   Appearing as Disneyesque castles, rococco palaces,
accommo-   ships or some other fantastic design, there are Japan's
dation   love hotels, where couples check in for the night or day. These offer western accommodation at not too high a price. Members of a foreign orchestra visiting Japan some time ago were inadvertently put up at a love hotel by the organizers. Their tour was a huge success!

Traditional   The word *ryokan* is usually translated as 'Japanese
accommo-   inn'. There is a wide range of ryokan. At the top end
dation   of the scale they are regal and at least as expensive as
Ryokan   the top international hotels. Many foreigners find it difficult to book into the best ryokan, as they are so heavily booked in advance by the Japanese.

Ryokan are often sited at *onsen* (hot springs), and it is the custom on arrival to sip green tea, take a hot bath and then put on *yukata* or the thicker winter variety, *tanzen* or *dotera*. Dinner is served either in your room or in the dining-room where guests conventionally wear yukata and slippers. Ryokan provide some of Japan's finest traditional cooking and the service is excellent. In the evening the maid puts out the bedding for you, folding it away in the morning.

The JNTO are keen that foreigners should try out ryokan, and have produced several booklets on the subject. As the accommodation is Japanese, you must leave your shoes at the entrance to the building and change into the slippers provided. If you take a Japanese bath, you must follow convention by washing with soap outside the bath, and treat the bath itself as simply a place in which to soak and think.

If you wish to try another typically Japanese style of accommodation you should contact: *Minshuku*

Nihon Minshuku Center
10–1 Yurakucho
Chiyoda-ku
Tokyo
(tel. 216–6556)

The Centre is English-speaking and near the Tokyo TIC. It will book you into a *minshuku* or 'home accommodation'. Few of the 20,000 families opening their houses to guests in this way can speak English, although hosts are very keen to make their guests comfortable. A minshuku provides breakfast and an evening meal, and the cooking is excellent, reflecting the great regional variety of the Japanese cuisine. Prices are very reasonable.

Staying with a Japanese family is a good idea if you wish to experience something of the Japanese way of life. It may be that you can come to some arrangement, such as giving English lessons in return for room and board. Sometimes home stays work wonderfully and sometimes they don't, but the following advice may be useful. First, find out how your family lives and fall in with their ways; try to be tidy and offer to do a few chores. Second, always put rent in an envelope – the Japanese tend not to hand money over directly and frequently put a small gift in with their payments. Always pay rent in advance. Third, bring home ice-cream, cakes, etc. now and again, for the rent charged will probably be far from realistic.

'Out in the country First, there are *pensions*, cheap (though a bit more expensive than minshuku), where you have a room in a Japanese home, and are treated as a paying guest, rather than one of the family. You can get information directly by calling the Japanese Pension Association Reservations Centre in Tokyo (295–6333).

In Japan's national parks there are People's Lodges (*Kokumin Shukusha*) and National Vacation Villages (*Kokumin Kyuka mura*). The number of places available is strictly limited, so visitors may not be able to get in to stay there. There are also cycling inns stationed along Japan's cycling trails, and some Buddhist temples offer accommodation and vegetarian cooking. Ask the TIC for information on all these.

Youth hostels Anyone can stay at a youth hostel in Japan. It is easiest if you take your International Youth Hostels' Federation card with you. If you need to get a card in Japan, go to the YH National Headquarters near the Youth Hostel in Ichigaya (Tokyo) or to the YH desk at the Sogo Department Store (Yurakucho, Tokyo), the Keio Department Store (Shinjuku, Tokyo) or the Sogo Department Store (Shinsaibashi, Osaka).

Youth hostels offer the cheapest accommodation. They are of a high standard and very often set in beautiful surroundings. Their house rules (lights-out time, latest return times, etc.), once decidedly Victorian, are now increasingly more relaxed.

Other cheap accommo- dation In the last few years there has been an increase in the availability of cheap basic accommodation (western and Japanese) specifically designed to help foreign visitors managing on tight budgets. No meals or services are offered. Usually there are weekly and monthly rates. The TIC has details and information can also be found in the monthly *Tokyo Journal* and *Kansai Time Out*. The names of two such places are Kimi Ryokan, Tokyo (971–3766, 985–0230), and Yuhara Hotel, Kyoto (075–371–9583).

The 'no tipping' rule in Japan includes hotels, though a number of foreigners have been giving tips in the larger hotels and upsetting this excellent custom. Hotels and ryokan levy a service charge of between 10 and 15 per cent, included in the bill.

Tax is levied on a bill of over 5,000 yen per person per night (including service charge) at the rate of 10 per cent after 2,500 yen has been deducted.

Service charges and tax

If you are offered accommodation as part of your work contract, take it. Accommodation is expensive in Japan, particularly in Tokyo.

Long-stay accommodation

Advertisements for expensive flats and houses can be found in the *Japan Times* and for more down market properties in the *Tokyo Journal* and *Kansai Time Out*.

A Japanese agency will offer a wide range of rented accommodation. Agencies are numerous, and those offering an English-speaking service advertise in the English newspapers. It is customary to pay one month's rent in advance plus two months' rent as 'key money'. This is used to cover damages and is returned two or three years later.

It is very good to have a Japanese friend help you look for accommodation – it is amazing how one materializes!

When looking at potential homes, think about:

1 The distance from the station and the time it will take to get to work – access to a station is very important in Japan.
2 The location of shops and schools for children (if relevant).
3 Heating – not much to be done here. In Japan central heating is a novelty and expensive. Japanese homes have gas fires and very often *kotatsu* – electric heaters under a low table covered with a blanket. Remember that winters are cold in Japan.
4 Inspect the toilet and bathroom – could you manage with Japanese style facilities, i.e. with squat loos and bathrooms where you have to light a gas boiler to get hot water? Be prepared, at the very least, for a small bath where your chin will rest on your knees.

5 Visit an apartment in the evening as well as day time to gauge the noise level when neighbours are at home.

Very, very few Japanese households have maids or home helps and you must expect to do all the housework yourself (though in central Tokyo there are maid service agencies as in America, and caterers who can be called in for dinners, etc.) If you plan to take a nanny or maid with you, don't forget to apply for a work permit early on in your pre-travel preparations (allow at least two months).

A Japanese home

Japanese lifestyles have been changing fast. A large number of people now live in apartments and some in western-style houses. In the past 30 or 40 years the Japanese have not tended to build larger houses, but their homes are now better equipped and they are keen to have *all* the latest gadgets, even if this means keeping the washing machine outside the front door. However, many aspects of traditional Japanese home life have been preserved despite the modern accommodation, and it is rare to find a Japanese home completely as it would be in the West.

Genkan

The *genkan* or entrance hall has always been an important feature of the Japanese home. Visitors used to step up from the genkan into the house. The elevation of the rooms allowed air to circulate and helped to cope with humidity in summer. Today the genkan is much more like a hallway, and is the place where, entering the house, the family changes from shoes into slippers. A stock of slippers for guests is kept by the entrance. It is a place of welcome, and invariably contains a flower arrangement and perhaps a picture. When visitors depart everyone comes to the genkan to bow farewell.

A traditional living-room

The treatment of space in Japan is often quite different to that in the West. The main room is used for several functions – living, eating and sleeping, and the furnishings tend to be basic: cushions or *zabuton* around a low table. (The table with a heater under-

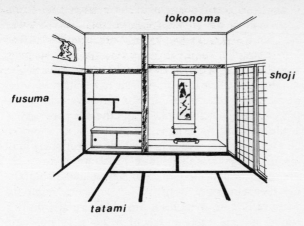

A traditional Japanese living-room
© Hiroshi Umemura 1985

neath (a kotatsu) is the traditional way to keep warm in winter.) The distinctive features are linked to considerations of space: *oshiire* or closets in which bedding, clothes, etc. can be stored during the day; and *fusuma* (sliding doors) on the oshiire or room dividers. Fusuma are often beautifully decorated and, taken off their runners, can change a room instantly.

The *tokonoma* or recess originally measured one tatami mat in depth. This contained the principal flower arrangement in the living-room and invariably had a scroll painting (*kakejiku*) or piece of pottery, in front of which a guest was seated. Flowers, pots, dolls, etc. are placed much lower in Japan than in the West, sometimes just off the floor. (Remember that a Japanese room should be viewed from a sitting position, and that the optimum eye-level will be thought of differently in the East and West.) Most Japanese homes still have a tokonoma, though it may be smaller than one tatami in depth. *Tokonoma*

Small and functional and not for dining or entertaining in. *The kitchen*

Traditionally, the Japanese built with wood and paper, materials suited to the climate and to earth- *Materials* quakes. (A carpenter might have built an entire house.) Now the Japanese use concrete, bricks, glass, etc., but wood and paper happily still have their place. For example, there are *shoji*, heavy rice papers stretched on a wooden frame. These are remarkably durable, and the paper only needs to be changed once a year. Shoji often stand next to windows, taking the place of curtains in the West, and the rice paper gives a pleasant diffused light. There are also bamboo curtains, *sudare*, which give shade in summer, and *amado*, heavy wooden shutters that are drawn each evening (though modern houses have metal shutters on the windows). Finally, no Japanese home is without *tatami*, mats made from dried grass, on the floor – no one walks on tatami in shoes. Tatami feels warm in winter and cool in summer, and new tatami has a pleasant smell. The Japanese still measure rooms by the number of tatami they will hold. A mat is generally 1.8 by 0.9 metres. Even the 'most modern' homes still tend to keep what they call the *tatamino-ma* – a room with tatami on the floor and with Japanese furnishings.

Decoration The Japanese are fond of reflecting the passing of seasons through interior decoration, changing pictures, wall hangings, etc. to suit the seasonal mood. Flower arrangements always represent the time of year or a particular festival.

Aspect The Japanese have always liked south-facing houses to feel the benefit of the winter sun. They like to be able to dry their washing outside and air *futon* (mattresses) on their terraces throughout the year.

The garden The garden has always been a valued part of a Japanese home – rarely treated as a place for children to let off steam, but usually as a beautiful place to look at, and, if large enough, to stroll in. Japanese homes without gardens frequently find some substitute – pots of plants or *bonsai* usually arranged on shelves.

Money matters

Japan is a cash society *par excellence*. The Japanese trust money (rather than other means of payment) and pay for quite large items in cash, so don't be surprised if Japanese friends and acquaintances *never* use cheques or credit cards.

There are two reasons for this. First, Japan is an extremely safe country. (People are even in the habit of returning lost cash.) Second, cash dispensers are readily available. Banks make them accessible on just about every main street, and they operate between 9 am and 6 pm on weekdays and between 9 am and 1 pm on Saturdays. Inside banks, halls equipped with tables and chairs are put aside simply for cash dispensers. Department stores generally have dispensers supplied by all the main banks.

The Japanese currency

The unit of currency in Japan is the *yen*. The abbreviation, ¥, usually precedes the designated sum (as ¥500, for instance). At the time of writing, there are ¥220 to £1 and ¥130 to $1. However, as the exchange rates are unlikely to remain stable it is worth checking them daily.

Coins

There are six coins: ¥1, ¥5, ¥10, ¥50, ¥100, ¥500. The ¥1 and ¥5 coins have little value and mostly end up in offertory boxes at shrines and temples. Because the ¥500 is comparatively new, shop assistants and others may make a point of showing it to you when giving change, in order to avoid confusion.

Notes

There are four notes: ¥500, ¥1,000, ¥5,000 and ¥10,000. (Newly designed versions of the last three were introduced in 1984.)

You may be mildly surprised not to see the emperor's portrait on the currency (or on stamps). It was once thought disrespectful to place the emperor's image where it could be thumbed and handled and this belief continues today.

Handling cash with discretion

Although cash is acceptable everywhere in Japan, you will need to be discreet with it on occasion. For example, when paying for certain services (for example, for private tuition) it is best to put the cash into an envelope, rather than place it directly into someone's hand. Next to the tills at banks there are supplies of free cash envelopes for you to take and use for such payments. These envelopes carry the symbol of the bank and sometimes look fairly smart. You can also buy special envelopes from stationers in which to put money as a present.

Contrasting with this discretion, Japanese shopkeepers often make a fan with notes given in change in order to show customers exactly what they are to receive.

Banks and banking

There are many commercial banks in Japan. The biggest are:

Daiichi Kangyo	Saitama
Fuji	Tokyo
Mitsubishi	Taiyo Kobe
Mitsui	Sanwa
Sumitomo	

Notice that the names of some of the banks (for example, Mitsubishi, Mitsui, Sumitomo) are also the names of large trading and industrial enterprises. This is, or course, a characteristic of the Japanese economy: the banking side of an enterprise raises the capital needed by the industrial side.

It is fairly prestigious to work in a bank in Japan. You can therefore expect good service, and will rarely need to wait for attention. If your papers take some time to sort out, you will be seated in an armchair until they are ready.

Banking hours

Banks are open between 9 am and 3 pm on weekdays and between 9 am and 12 pm on Saturdays.

A foreign visitor can easily open a bank account in Japan. It is advisable to take a Japanese friend or acquaintance along with you on the first visit, although you will probably get the services of the best English-speaker in the bank thereafter. Banks offer a full service. They are polite and attentive – part of the Japanese way, but also perhaps a result of fierce competition.

Opening an account

People do use cheques in Japan, but they are not common. More often, people open accounts at department stores, while banks automatically pay all utility bills. (They will even inform the gas, electricity and telephone companies when you are leaving the country.)

Cheques

These can be cashed in banks and hotels but not often in shops or restaurants. Banks give the best rates.

You will get the quickest service in Japan by using currency that is familiar everywhere, so take travellers' cheques in dollars.

Travellers' cheques

These are not widely used in Japan, although American Express are trying to persuade the Japanese to acquire the habit. The international credit cards acceptable in Japan include American Express, Diners Club, MasterCard and Visa, and most large shops, restaurants and hotels take them. (For British travellers, using an Access card may be difficult, but if you point out the MasterCard symbol it is usually accepted.)

Credit cards

Overdrafts and loans are negotiated on an individual basis, but this is not the usual way to acquire extra finance. An ordinary person will borrow money by offering his or her life insurance cover, etc. as surety, or by negotiating a loan with an employer. For an enormous purchase, such as a house, an employee will generally receive a low-interest loan from the employer.

Overdrafts and loans

Investments Banks offer low returns on investments, so a large number of people in Japan play the stock-market. Securities are generally a good investment. (JETRO offers a free booklet 'Investing in Japan', giving advice to the would-be foreign investor.) For the ordinary Japanese person, however, extra life insurance is the most popular form of investment.

Mail and telephones

The symbol for a post office is a T with a bar across the top. The symbol is used with post codes: T182 indicates postal district 182, for example. **Mail** *Post Offices*

Opening times:

Weekdays   9 am to 5 pm
Saturdays   9 am to 12.30 pm first and fourth Saturdays. Main Post Office, Tokyo, 9 am to 3.30 pm Saturdays.

Communication at a post office is not difficult. The clerks know enough English to deal with inquiries and will write the cost of a letter or parcel on the spot where you place the stamp(s). (The only possible difficulty is that post office staff tend to assume that foreigners will want to mail all letters overseas.)

You can also buy stamps and get information on postal services from hotel clerks.

Mailboxes are red and free-standing and can be found on street corners. There are usually two boxes: in Tokyo the right-hand one is for city mail only and the left for all other mail. If you feel doubtful, appeal for help. *Mailboxes*

First-class letter, standard size *Domestic mail rates*

up to 25 g	¥60
up to 50 g	¥70
express letter	¥200
registered letter	¥350
postcards	¥40

First-class letters take a day and the postal service is generally very good, although there is only one delivery each day (Monday–Saturday).

Overseas mail For letters and cards there are three zones: Zone 1 –
rates East Asia and Oceania; Zone 2 – the USA, Canada,
Central America and the West Indies; Zone 3 –
Europe, Africa, South America, West Asia, the Near
East, the Middle East and the USSR. The rates are as
follows:

Zone	Letters Airmail (10 g)	Seamail (20 g)	Postcards Airmail	Seamail	Aero-grammes
1	¥130	¥70	¥90	¥50	¥120
2	¥150	¥110	¥100	¥80	¥120
3	¥170	¥110	¥110	¥80	¥120

For each additional 10 g or fraction on airmail
letters add ¥70 for letters to Zone 1, ¥90 for letters to
Zone 2, ¥110 for Zone 3. For letters sent express mail
add an extra charge of ¥300 to the price; add ¥350 for
registered mail and ¥250 for advice of delivery.

Letters and cards take about five days to reach
Europe or North America by airmail.

Cheap rates To qualify for a special printed-matter rate to places
overseas your parcel must be left open at one end. (It
will be inspected at the post office.)

Christmas and New Year cards may be mailed at a
cheap rate if you write nothing but your signature on
them and if you do not seal the envelopes. (The cheap
rate applies to Christmas cards sent abroad and to
New Year cards sent within Japan. The Japanese do
not celebrate Christmas, but recognize that others
do!)

An international business mail service is available at
post offices where prior arrangements have been
made for official communications, data and commercial papers. The zones are the same as those for letters
and postcards, and the rates are as follows:

Zone 1   ¥2,170 up to 500 g   ¥300 for each
additional 100 g

| Zone 2 | ¥2,490 up to 500 g | ¥360 for each additional 100 g |
| Zone 3 | ¥2,820 up to 500 g | ¥430 for each additional 100 g |

The Japanese Post Office and American Express operate a *poste restante* service.

Poste restante

Parcels for destinations abroad have to be sent from major post offices (for example, Tokyo Central Post Office, near Tokyo Station). Parcels must be no more than 1 metre in length and must weigh no more than 10 kilograms. If you are planning to send a large parcel, it is advisable to consult the post office first. Alternatively, most department stores are quite happy to post your purchases for you.

Parcels

The rates are based on the same zones as those for letters and postcards. Here are some examples:

| | Seamail | | Airmail | |
Zone	up to 1 kg	each additional kg	up to 500 g	each additional 500 g
1	¥1,800	¥400	¥2,600	¥1,000
2	¥1,750	¥600	¥2,400	¥1,000
3	¥2,300	¥800	¥2,900	¥1,050

Tokyo Postal Services Bureau issues a complex but comprehensive booklet entitled *Postal Charges*, which is available free on application.

Finding a telephone in Japan should not be a problem. Most hotel rooms are equipped with phones, and they are also available in post offices, department stores and coffee shops, at news stands and on station platforms. They are always clean, gleaming and in perfect working order – a shock for visiting Londoners and New Yorkers.

Telephones

International calls
You can dial many countries direct from Japan, among them America and countries in Europe. But the number of public phones from which you can make and pay for international calls is limited. These are found at airports and main railway stations, and are yellow and green (see *Using public telephones*). They take a maximum of 9 ¥100 coins. Alternatively, dial the KDD operator and make a reverse charge call.

All international calls are handled by Kokusai Denshin Denwa (KDD). KDD operators speak excellent (American) English – for the sake of clarity, say 'zero' rather than '0' or 'nought', and 'collect call' rather than 'reverse charges'. For information about KDD services, call the KDD Information Centre, Tokyo 250–5111.

For the international KDD operator, dial 0051. (Residents will find it much cheaper to arrange for KDD to install a telephone with direct international dialling.)

Station-to-station calls cost less than person-to-person calls. Three-minute station calls to Australia, Canada and USA cost approximately ¥2,160 and to European countries about ¥2,490.

Time differences
When making an international call, bear in mind the following differences in time between Japan and cities in other countries:

Auckland	+3 hours	Los Angeles	−17 hours
Bangkok	−2	New York	−14
Chicago	−15	Paris	−8
Hong Kong	−1	Singapore	−1½
London	−8 (−9)	Sydney	+1

International telegrams and telex
Contact KDD, Tokyo 0051. The cost per word transmitted to the USA is ¥118 and to Europe ¥192.

Some hotels operate special services for businessmen – for example, rooms equipped with telex, typewriters, stationery, telephones, etc., and an assistant or two to help.

Telephone calls within Japan
The Nippon Telegraph and Telephone Corporation (NTT), which became a private company in 1985,

operates the domestic telephone system in Japan. Although some NTT employees speak English, it is advisable to call on the help of a Japanese friend in any negotiations with the company.

Late evening is the best time to make long-distance calls within Japan. Between 7 pm and 8 am calls to places over 60 kilometres away cost 40 per cent less than the standard rate. Between 9 pm and 6 am calls to places more than 320 kilometres away cost 50 per cent less than the standard rate. On Sundays and holidays there is an additional concession: between 6 am and 9 pm there is a 40 per cent reduction on calls to places more than 60 kilometres away. *Reduced rates*

There are no directories in English. If you need to find a number, ask someone Japanese to look it up for you. *Directories*

There are several different types of public telephone in Japan. The four colours – red/pink, pale blue, yellow, green – indicate the different quantities and denominations of coins that you may insert to make a call, depending on how long you intend to speak. The numbers on the dials are arabic, so they will be entirely familiar to you. *Using public telephones*

Red telephones (found in restaurants, for example), will take up to six ¥10 coins.

Pale-blue telephones (found in street booths) will take up to ten ¥10 coins. (Both of these are good for local calls only.)

Yellow telephones (found in call boxes etc.) will take nine ¥100 coins or ten ¥10 coins.

Green telephones accept magnetized telephone cards as well as ¥10 and ¥100 coins.

Pick up the receiver and insert the coin(s) (¥10 for local calls, ¥100 for long-distance). Wait for the dialling tone (a continuous hum) and then dial the number. A *beep* during the conversation signals the last ¥10 or the remaining ten seconds (on green phones only). Insert more coins if you wish to continue speaking. Any coins not used will be returned automatically at the end of the call. *Dialling the number*

28   Mail and telephones

The engaged signal An unmistakable *bao-bao* sound indicates that the number you are calling is engaged.

Answering the telephone The Japanese equivalent of 'hello' is *moshi-moshi*, though many Japanese say instead, 'Hai, Smith desu' ('Yes, this is Mr Smith'). It is probably best for foreign visitors to answer the phone with 'hello', otherwise the caller may continue to speak in Japanese.

Having a telephone installed Visit your local NTT office between 9 am and 4 pm on weekdays and between 9 am and 12 pm on Saturdays. You will need to take with you your certificate of Alien Registration, your passport and one other item that will serve to identify you (your driving licence, for example).

Your telephone will be installed about a week after you have applied for it. Make sure that someone is at home to let in the telephone engineers.

Emergency advice

Fire

Dial 119 (Japanese-speaking service only). If there is no one Japanese at hand to help with the language, dial the KDD operator on 0051. Ask the operator to relay your message to the emergency services.

Police

Dial 110 (Japanese-speaking service only). In the absence of any Japanese speaker, dial 0051, or find the nearest police box.

Police boxes are a great Japanese invention. Each box is manned constantly and is responsible for a very small area. The police on duty make regular courtesy calls on the residents in their block and talk to the locals about any new or unusual occurrences in the district. Foreign residents will be well known to the local police unit.

Police boxes are in the tradition of a highly supervised society. During the Edo period (1603–1868) no one could move from their locality; everyone had to speak with the local accent so they could be readily identified; people were encouraged to report on their neighbours; and there were files on everyone. Indeed the Japanese still accept a degree of state supervision that would be generally unacceptable in the West.

Ambulance

Dial 119 (Japanese-speaking service only). If there is no one Japanese present to make the call for you, it might be best to contact an English-speaking hospital instead (see below). Otherwise dial 0051.

Hospitals

There are a number of very well-known hospitals with English-speaking staff:

St Luke's International Hospital, Tokyo   (541–5151)
Tokyo Medical and Surgical Clinic   (436–3028)

Yodogawa Christian Hospital, Osaka   (06–322–2250)
Kobe Adventist Hospital   (078–981–0161)
Kobe Kaisei International Hospital   (078–871–5201)
Nihon Baptist Hospital, Kyoto   (075–781–5191)

Dental care St Luke's International Hospital in Tokyo has a fine dental department. There is a dental office in the Hilton Hotel, Tokyo (581–4511, ext. 72). Two other well known sources of dental care in Tokyo are John Besford, No. 32, Mori Building (431–4225), and the Olympia Ohba Dental Clinic (409–7155).

Pharmacies See page 63 for names of pharmacies with large stocks of imported drugs and toiletries. Local pharmacies, however, will have a large number of familiar products on their shelves, remedies for colds and headaches for example.

Oculists Ask for advice at any large hotel. The TIC will also help with names and addresses.

Counselling Organizations that will help with your problems or worries are:

International Social Services, Tokyo   (711–5551)
Tokyo Community Counselling Service (434–4992)
Tokyo English Life Line   (264–4347)
Alcoholics Anonymous   (431–8534)

Gas and electricity There is no single emergency number for help here: the number you should ring will depend on the ward (district) in which you live. Residents should consult neighbours or the janitor.

Lost property If you leave something in a train, on the subway or in a taxi, check in the appropriate places, but don't lose heart if you don't find it. After a few days all lost property is returned to the Central Lost and Found Office of the Metropolitan Police Board, 1–9–11 Koraku, Bunkyo-ku, Tokyo (814–4151).

Typhoons The typhoon season is June–October. The US forces radio station (FEN) gives typhoon warnings, as

American military personnel have to be alerted. There are three conditions for typhoon warnings:

condition 1   winds of 50 knots or more anticipated within 12 hours;
condition 2   winds of 50 knots or more anticipated within 24 hours;
condition 3   winds of 50 knots or more anticipated within 48 hours.

If you do hear of a typhoon alert, *don't panic*. Typhoons rarely hit Tokyo as anything more than a high wind. But if a typhoon is fairly imminent, take the following steps:

Build up your food stocks.
Fill up containers with water or buy bottled mineral water.
Close the windows.
Fasten the shutters.
Make sure that you have a torch (flashlight).
Bring in everything that is outside the house or flat.
Garage your car.
Cancel all travel arrangements.
Do not use elevators in case of a power cut.

Earthquakes

Earthquakes can occur at any time – and, of course, there is no warning. The Japanese always keep a stock of emergency food and drink at home and take care to have lamps etc. available.

In a serious earthquake the gravest danger is from fire. Take the following steps:

Switch off the gas and do not use matches until you are sure that all is well.
Open the door to your house or flat in case it jams during the quake.
Stay still, in one room, but well away from glass.
If you happen to be driving, pull in and switch off the engine of your car.

The Shinkansen (railway) network closes down automatically in the event of a major earthquake.

Japan is efficiently geared to cope with earthquakes. Each district has a 'green' area to which you may evacuate. The Tokyo Metropolitan Government issues a booklet entitled *Protecting Yourself in an Earthquake*, which can be obtained from your ward office or from your embassy or chamber of commerce.

Getting about

If, as seems fairly certain, you have to ask directions from someone Japanese, speak slowly, clearly and simply. Instead of: 'Could you possibly tell me the way to Shinjuku Station?', say, 'Shinjuku Station, please.'

Asking for directions

Most Japanese know some English, but choose your source with care. Young people recently or still at school are most likely to be familiar with the language, as are businessmen, who generally have received a good education, and who may, in addition, use English in their work. There are police boxes in towns and cities throughout Japan, and directions or advice can be sought there too.

Useful Japanese words are:

migi	right	*ue ni*	above
hidari	left	*koko*	here
massugu	straight on	*soko*	there
mukai ni	opposite	*asoko*	over there
mae ni	in front of	*kita*	north
tonari ni	next to	*minami*	south
ushiro ni	behind	*higashi*	east
shita ni	below	*nishi*	west

On foot

It is wise to know where you are going before you set out. Unless you are in a small town, don't just wander. You may easily lose your way. If you are visiting anything other than a national landmark, ask someone Japanese to write down the name of the place and location in Japanese to show people if you get lost. Hotel and business cards are also useful when trying to get directions.

Don't jay-walk (British visitors beware!). Always cross streets as and where instructed.

Public transport

Public transport is excellent in Japan. It is clean, punctual and safe (though occasionally intoxicated businessmen on late-night trains want to practise their English, but nothing more). Even if you are able regularly to afford a taxi, it is not always the quickest way to travel. In Tokyo, for example, one can often do a journey by train in a fraction of the time it would take by taxi. The public transport system closes down at about midnight.

Trains

There is a publicly owned rail and subway (or underground) system in Japan called the Japanese National Railway (JNR). There are also a large number of private rail and subway lines. Private lines in Japan are invariably owned by large corporations and run at a profit (although fares are generally lower than those charged by the JNR). Some private railway lines terminate at a department store owned by the corporation.

The Japanese rail pass

The JNR has a rail pass similar to the Britrail and Eurail passes for foreign travellers in Britain and Europe.

Type	7 days	14 days	21 days
Ordinary car	¥25,000	¥41,000	¥53,000
Green car	¥35,000	¥58,000	¥76,000
(former first-class car)			

Rail passes are half price for children 11 years of age and under. A voucher for the pass has to be bought outside Japan. (JNTO offices will tell you where it is sold.) The voucher can then be exchanged for the pass at any major railway station in Japan. The pass, which enables you to use all JNR rail, subway and ferry services freely, is excellent value, and people organizing their own tour of Japan should not think twice about acquiring one.

The Shinkansen

The most famous of Japan's trains is the high-speed train known as the bullet-train or *Shinkansen*. These run on JNR services and are not used by private companies. There are two types of Shinkansen: the *hikari*, which makes the minimum number of stops on a journey, and the *kodama* which stops more frequently.

The Shinkansen usually has sixteen cars; with the hikari the first five have non-reserved seats, the rest are reserved. It is advisable to book a seat. With a JNR pass there is no charge; otherwise it costs ¥500. Shinkansen bookings are made at the ticket window with the sign of the reclining pin man above.

Smoking is allowed throughout most of the Shinkansen. However, the air-conditioning is excellent, and the non-smoker is not likely to feel uncomfortable in the smoking part of the train.

The Shinkansen is fast and luxurious. A wide selection of food and drinks are served throughout the journey. There is also a telephone on board.

Ticket machines

You may often have to buy a train/subway ticket from a machine. If there is no route map in English, telling you the fare, ask someone's help: for example, 'Shinjuku station', said with rising intonation and a worried look turning into a smile, clearly indicates your difficulty. If this fails, buy the cheapest ticket and pay the difference at your destination. This is legal in Japan, and there are fare adjustment offices for that purpose at most main stations.

Platforms

If you are uncertain which platform your train leaves from, try the same appeal used at the ticket machine, this time approaching the ticket-collector. The reply may be rather formal and restrained, but there is a fund of goodwill there. (Recently a fulsome apology appeared in a Japanese newspaper expressing the regret of a JNR employee for misdirecting a foreign visitor at the station.)

Casting your eye around the platform or track, there are several things you may notice: on Shinkansen platforms, signs showing exactly where each car stops; circles/arrows on other platforms, which show where subway/train doors will open – a queue forms at these spots; a serrated yellow band near the edge of platforms and down stairs to guide the blind; various facilities such as drinking fountains, ashtrays on stands and small mirrors.

All Japanese stations have toilets – some reasonable, some rather grim. There is usually no charge.

Level crossings These are common in big cities, especially in Tokyo,
because the railway network is so extensive. A
flashing light and loud warning noise indicate that a
train is due and these continue until the barrier is
raised again. The barrier comes down 7 seconds after
the initial warning. During that time pedestrians may
cross over (quickly) but cars *must* stop. (The barrier,
by the way, is a light bamboo pole!)

Rush hours Rush hours in Japan fall between 8 and 9.30 am and 5
and 6.30 pm. They should be avoided unless you
want to confirm whether or not white-gloved station
staff really do push passengers into the train. (They
do.)

Other means An internal flight might not cost much more than a
of transport Shinkansen ticket, and flying is something for the
Planes businessman (or woman) to check out. Three airlines
operate domestic routes: Japan Air Lines (JAL), All
Nippon Airways (ANA) and Toa Domestic Airlines
(TDA).

Sea As befits a country of islands Japan has an enormous
number of ferries. The TIC have a great deal of
information about services which are all extremely
good value. Most tourists who take to the water do so
on the Inland Sea. Both the Kansai Steamship
Company and the Setonaikai Steamship Company
(*Setonaikai* means Inland Sea) operate leisure cruises
on the Inland Sea. Holders of the Japan Rail Pass can
use the JNR ferries free of charge, and can reach such
faraway places as Kyushu, Hokkaido and Okinawa.

Bus You really need a Japanese friend's introduction to a
bus route, as the route will be written in Japanese
letters on the front of the bus. The method of paying
varies; you pay either on entering or leaving. Some of
the buses on which you pay as you leave mark up
fares on an electronic indicator at the front. All buses
have a taped route message announcing each stop and
standing is definitely allowed.

Inter-city express buses are much cheaper than the Shinkansen. The most popular route is that between Kanto and Kansai. (Buses depart from outside Tokyo station.) Some people travel at night and sleep on the bus. (Some people of course travel in the day and sleep on the bus.)

Taxi

Taxi fares in Tokyo start at roughly 470 yen. Taxis take a maximum of five passengers, and as the same fare is charged for one or more passengers, it is a good idea for a small group of people to hire one taxi between them. In ordinary taxis you should not tip the driver. (I had a tip given back to me when I first took a taxi in Japan.) But if you hire a car for a day with a chauffeur, you should sometimes give a tip, especially if you think the chauffeur has gone out of his way to please.

Somewhat contrary to usual colour conventions, when the two lights (usually on the windscreen of a taxi) are red, it means that the car is free; when they are green it is booked. The Japanese stop a taxi by stretching out their arms and fluttering their fingers up and down. This gesture in general means summoning someone or something to you, and is not, as is sometimes thought by westerners, a refined goodbye.

Watch out for taxi doors, which generally open and close automatically.

Driving

The Japanese drive on the left. Road signs are the same as those used in Europe.

It may not seem worth bothering to drive in Japan. The costs of driving are high, and the public transport system is reliable and extensive. However, a tourist can drive in the country with an international driver's licence; a resident needs a Japanese driver's licence. This is fairly easy to obtain so long as you already hold a licence from your own country. For information and an excellent booklet, *Rules of the Road*, contact:

The Japan Automobile Federation (JAF)
3–5–8, Shiba-Koen
Minato-ku
Tokyo
(tel. 436–2811)

For those who wish to hire a car, there are many rent-a-car companies in Japan offering a variety of facilities and rate systems. You can book directly, or through a travel agent or your hotel.

A point to note: drinking and driving is forbidden in Japan and punishable with imprisonment.

Bicycle   Many Japanese people ride bicycles, and some pavements are divided into two lanes, one for pedestrians and one for cyclists. Railway stations are frequently surrounded by a forest of parked bicycles. You can hire bicycles in resort areas like Karuizawa and have a lot of fun. Many resident foreigners buy bikes or motorcycles for their stay. Japan is an honest nation, but bicycles may stray, and it is always a good idea to lock your bike.

The address of the Japan Cycling Association is:

c/o Maeda Industry Co. Ltd.
3–8–1 Ueno
Taito-ku
Tokyo
(tel. 583–5628)

As a member of the association you can take a bike on the train though you must provide the bike with a protective cover.

Hitching   This is not at all in the Japanese tradition. Foreigners who do hitch speak of the embarrassing kindness of Japanese drivers, but whether you can count on this as a means of getting around is less certain.

Organized   For information about organized tours visit the
tours   JNTO. The Japan Tourist Bureau (JTB) and Fujita Travel have a wide selection of tours, and they generally have desks in the lobbies of large hotels. Organized tours take all the fuss out of travelling around Japan, but perhaps the fuss is all part of the fun. Certainly you will pay more for a tour than you will travelling around on your own using public transport and staying in modest accommodation.

Eating . . .

Japanese food is much better known in the United States than it is in Europe, where it is relatively expensive and something of a novelty. Those who have not tried Japanese food before may be a little apprehensive, but there is no reason for this. Japanese cooking is tasty and among the most nutritious and healthy in the world.

Traditional Japanese cuisine depends on taking the freshest of ingredients and cooking them (usually) for a short time and with very few spices. Some famous Japanese dishes are not cooked at all – the best fish, for example, is thinly sliced and served raw as *sashimi*. Until the last century few Japanese were meat eaters. The basis of a typical meal was rice with vegetables or perhaps fish. Since Japan opened to the outside world there has been an invasion of every food imaginable, and the Japanese diet is now extremely varied. There

'It's an old Japanese recipe.'

Reproduced by courtesy of *Punch*

is a vast range of restaurants in Japan, from the traditional, serving an ancient and delicate cuisine, to the brashest hamburger outlet.

The most marked regional difference in food is between Kanto and Kansai. Kanto cuisine uses more soy sauce than Kansai, while the latter uses more salt. Yet despite some regional specialities, on the whole the style of cooking is the same everywhere, and the dishes mentioned in this section are available throughout Japan.

Where to eat The widest selection of restaurants can be found in the cities, but it is surprising how many restaurants there are even in small towns. Indeed today the Japanese are eating out more and more frequently. There is a large student population living away from home (especially in Tokyo), numerous salaried men (office employees) dining in restaurants, while families are always eating out (occasions when a huge fuss is made of the children).

A major problem for the visitor eating out in Japan is the fact that you can never count on a menu (or even the restaurant's name) being written in English. Nor can you take a dictionary along and translate the menu as you might, for example, in Europe!

However, that does not mean you should stick to the big hotels and the chains of western restaurants, where things are written in English. First, Japanese hospitality will come to your rescue, and you will receive all the help and attention you need. Second, many restaurants display sample dishes in the window so that clients can see at a glance what is on offer. (This custom actually grew up in the nineteenth century to help the Japanese identify new foods from the West!) In this way you can easily take the waiter or waitress outside and point to what you want if you cannot make it clear with words.

Department stores have a good range of restaurants on their upper floors and have sample cases outside (with prices). Keen to attract shoppers, prices in these restaurants are usually very competitive. When the department store closes at 7 or 7.30 pm the restaurants usually stay open, closing at about 10. The shopping arcades near railway stations also have a wide range of places to eat, while the restaurants found at the top of corporation buildings are certainly worth investigating. (Those on the west side of Shinjuku enjoy prodigious views over Tokyo.)

It is rather difficult to give precise categories of places to eat as the menu depends very much on the tastes and talents of the owner. Some of the most plentiful and inexpensive restaurants are the *soba-ya* or *soba* shops which specialize in noodle dishes. A bowl of steaming noodles (broth with a sort of pasta and vegetables) will cost only about a pound or so or a little more than a dollar. Soba-ya do not usually have sample cases outside; some recommendations of what you could ask for are given later. A soba-ya has a *noren* or slit curtain at the doorway, often with the bicycles or motorbikes used for home deliveries propped up outside.

Soba-ya

© John Weatherhill Inc.

Other cheap restaurants

There are many cheap Japanese restaurants which serve a variety of noodle dishes, other Japanese dishes and some western-style dishes. They generally have a sample case. Restaurants of this kind are sometimes called *shokudō*, which also means canteen. These and other inexpensive restaurants usually have a TV which is kept on all day and perhaps also a selection of magazines and newspapers for their clients.

Specialist restaurants

There are many restaurants which specialize in particular Japanese foods. The most celebrated are *sushi-ya* which serve *sushi* and *sashimi*. Sushi-ya are expensive (eating à la carte one must expect to pay ¥6,000 per person at least – however, suggestions for more economical sushi eating are given later). There are restaurants which specialize in *tempura* (*tempura-ya*), *tonkatsu* (*tonkatsu-ya*) and *yakitori* (*yakitori-ya*). There are many restaurants whose speciality is food cooked at the table, and these range from the inexpensive *okonomi-yaki* restaurants to the more pricey *teppan-yaki* restaurants.

Chinese restaurants

Japan also has inexpensive Chinese restaurants (invariably run by the Japanese) which serve noodle and rice dishes. These may have sample cases (and at the end of this chapter there are some suggestions of what is on offer). More expensive Chinese restaurants (run by the Chinese) offer the range of dishes to be found in western Chinese restaurants, and it is worth noting that these usually have menus written in English. Japan's biggest Chinatown is at Yokohama.

Other 'foreign' food restaurants

French and Italian are the best known of the European restaurants. There have always been many Korean restaurants and there are increasing numbers of Indian, Indonesian, Thai, Vietnamese and Cambodian ones (look in Shinjuku, Ikebukuro and Shibuya in Tokyo, for example).

Western restaurant chains (McDonald's, Kentucky Fried Chicken) which are in force in Japan have identical menus to those offered in America and Britain. At first the Japanese found the portions served in these restaurants too large to cope with, but now they have adapted completely!

A list of inexpensive dishes that can be tasted in *Final advice*
Japan, and the names of some of the famous but more
costly dishes, are given at the end of this chapter. It is
a good idea to go out with the intention of eating a
particular food, and if you cannot identify what you
want, ask for one of the dishes in this book.

The westerner should not have difficulty coping with **Times**
Japanese meal times. The Japanese eat lunch between
12 and 1 pm and eat in the evening anywhere between
6 and 8. It is a good idea to select your restaurant
before 8 in the evening as many smaller restaurants
close down at about 9 pm (particularly soba-ya).
Some restaurants on highways stay open 24 hours a
day.

There are no restaurants in Japan that forbid or **Smoking in**
restrict smoking, and the Japanese smoke during a **restaurants**
meal if so inclined.

A set meal at lunchtime consists of soup, a small **Set meals**
salad, meat or fish and bread or rice. (The choice
between bread or rice may seem odd, but it is
standard procedure in Japan.) Sometimes the set meal
is on offer in the evenings as well.
  The set meal is much cheaper than ordering
individual items. A set, B set, etc. is just how the
Japanese order. The restaurant will help you out if
you have any difficulties.

Some restaurants (Pizza Huts, for example) have a **Other deals**
help yourself buffet, and there are many *kissaten* or
coffee shops which serve light snacks throughout the
day.
  Coffee shops also often offer a breakfast set meal
until 11 am. This usually comprises coffee, toast and
egg and perhaps a salad, and costs roughly the same
amount as a cup of coffee. It is way below what you
would pay for breakfast in a hotel. Alternatively, you
could try a traditional Japanese breakfast, a very
nutritious start to the day! Helpings of *miso* soup,
fish, egg, *nori* (dried seaweed), *tsukemono* (pickled
vegetables), rice. There is green tea to drink, but no

coffee. Hotels offer a traditional or western breakfast, or a buffet with the two. Ryokan serve a traditional breakfast.

Customs and manners
Finding a table

As a general rule the cheaper the restaurant, the more usual it is to find and sit down at your own table, and at many places (for example, cheap Chinese restaurants), there is simply a counter with stools. At more expensive restaurants you will be shown to a table. Tables are usually normal height, although some traditional restaurants and hotels have low tables where you sit on tatami.

'Why do you have to be the only one to say he's uncomfortable?'

Drawing by Saxon; © 1963 The New Yorker Magazine, Inc.

Shoes on or off?

It is very much a case of watch others and do what they do, but there is no chance that you will be allowed into a restaurant where shoes are taboo, wearing shoes. Traditional Japanese restaurants will either have a tatami floor or an area of tatami, and in these places you must remove your shoes. In high class traditional Japanese restaurants you will be met at the door and there will be someone to help you take off and put on your shoes and to look after them while you are dining. The need for immaculate hosiery is, as we have said before, essential at all times!

Oshibori are hand towels given to you on sitting down at your table. They are hot in winter and usually cold in summer. Airlines throughout the world seem to have borrowed this idea from Japan. *At the table*

It is customary to be served iced water and/or green tea throughout your meal.

If you cannot manage chopsticks, do not be afraid to ask for a knife, fork or spoon (*naihu*, *fuōku*, *supūn* in Japanese!). But Japanese chopsticks (*hashi*) are not so difficult. They are shorter and more manageable than the Chinese variety. The hashi usually come in a paper wrapper and have to be pulled apart. There is a new (perhaps snobbish) trend to put the chopsticks back in their wrapper when you have finished eating. Some restaurants provide chopstick rests (*hashioki*), and a few top class places give them away to foreigners as souvenirs.

It is the custom to help yourself from the main dish with your chopsticks, and as Japanese food is usually cut up, you will not then touch anything that another person eats. Sometimes there are long serving chopsticks (*tori-bashi* or *sai-bashi*).

itadakimasu	literally 'I shall begin eating', but like *bon appetit* in spirit	*Things to say*
gochisosama or *gochisosama deshita*	'That was good', said by satisfied customers to the owner or waiter on leaving.	

If you are in someone's home, the above two expressions shoud be used, plus: '(*totemo, taihen*) *oishikatta desu*', meaning 'That was (exceedingly) delicious.'

Depending on where you are, you either pay the waiter directly or take the bill (often in a wallet or attached to a clipboard) to the cash desk by the exit. *Paying*

In a few places (tourist centres, stations, etc.) you may have to buy a ticket (*kippu* or *shokken*) for the meal beforehand.

Tipping There is no tipping in restaurants. Expensive restaurants usually have a 10 per cent service charge and a government tax is levied on bills above ¥2,500 per person.

Dishes
Familiar foods The following dishes are found in a wide variety of restaurants:

Sandoiichi (*sandwiches*)	Excellent in Japan, but about the same price as a set meal. Fillings are mostly familiar. A popular order is a 'mixed sandwich'. Often served in kissaten.
Karē raisu	Curried rice the Japanese way is inexpensive, plentiful and on sale throughout Japan. The curry is very mild.
Hanbāga suteiki	A hamburger in the shape of a steak, sometimes with a fried egg on top. It is served with rice or french fries. (The Japanese say french fries rather than chips.) On sale in many western-style and cheap Japanese restaurants.

Dishes served in western-style restaurants:

Pirahu and *doria*	Two popular rice dishes with small pieces of vegetables, meat and chicken.
Guratan	Just like macaroni cheese.
Beikon eggu	Alias eggs and bacon.
Bīhu shichu	A tasty beef stew, served with bread or rice.
Purin	A creme caramel – the most common dessert in Japan.

Japanese staples Rice is an important part of the Japanese diet, but not as important as it once was when it seemed to be equated with life itself. The Japanese produce all their own rice and do not like the rice of other countries at all. It really is very good. When cooked it comes out on the sticky side rather than as separate grains. It is often served at the end of a Japanese meal. If you want some before, or need a second helping, you can ask for it (*tempura*, for example, is very rich but usually served without rice until the end).

Soybeans. Japan imports her soybeans from the American mid-west, and they also play an important part in the Japanese diet. The soybeans may be made into a paste, *miso*, from which Japanese make their favourite soup, *misoshiru*. Soysauce, *shooyu*, is on every dining-table. Bean curd, *tofu*, which looks like a soft creamish cake, is found in many dishes and eaten on its own.

Noodles are to the Japanese as pasta is to the Italians, and they taste very much the same. There are two types of Japanese noodles: *soba*, made from buckwheat flour and slightly brown in colour; and *udon*, made from white flour. There are also Chinese noodles called *kansui* (one of the ingredients is a mineral water called *kansui*).

The soba mAn who strUck it rich

© John Weatherhill Inc.

Eaten in *soba-ya* or Japanese noodle shops, noodle dishes are served piping hot and are slurped vigorously. They are eaten in the cheapest places. No napkins are provided, and newcomers are well advised to have a few tissues in their pockets!

Some noodle dishes

Noodles are excellent value, tasty and filling. You might be lucky enough to come across *jika sei udon/soba* or *teuchi-udon* or *tenobe-soba*, which is home-made soba or udon.

Yakumi	Many noodle dishes come with a small side dish, *yakumi*, containing a mixture of seven spices (*shichimi*) and shredded leeks (*naganegi*). It is customary to put the yakumi in with the noodles at the outset and stir them around.
Kake soba/udon	The basic noodle dish – noodles in bouillon.

The following are served in soba-ya only:

Kitsune soba/udon	Kake soba/udon plus fried *tofu* (*abura-age* or *age*), leeks and slices of *kamaboko* (neutral-tasting fish meat); *kitsune* means fox. The fox's favourite food is supposed to be abura-age!
Tanuki udon/soba	Kake plus fried *tenkasu* (pieces of fried batter), sometimes with leeks and kamaboko. *Tanuki* means racoon or cunning fellow.
Tsukimi udon/soba	Kake with kamaboko, dried seaweed (*nori*) spinach and egg. *Tsukimi* means moon watching and refers to the egg floating on the surface.
Tempura udon/soba	Kake with a few vegetables, and *tempura* – usually a couple of fried shrimps.
Nabe-yaki udon	*Nabe* means pot and *yaki* means cooked. Accordingly, you are served with an individual pot containing shrimp tempura, mushroom, egg, spinach and bamboo (*takenoko*).

Okame udon/soba	Kake plus kamaboko, mushrooms, bamboo and one or two wheat cakes called *fu*. *Okame* refers to a Japanese mask with a round face, low nose and high cheeks – thus a rather comical dish.
Mori soba and *zaru soba*	Eaten in summer, cold soba piled on oblong slatted boxes, and dunked in a dip (*tsuyu*) and yakumi before eating.

Dishes available both in soba-ya and cheap Chinese restaurants:

Rāmen	Chinese noodles are highly popular, served in bouillon with bamboo shoots, spinach and some or all of the following: leeks, fish cake (*naruto*), pork, ham.
Cha-shu-men	Chinese noodles with slices of pork on top, plus some or all of: spinach, leeks and Chinese bamboo.
Yaki soba	Broiled soba with shredded vegetables. This dish is sold at street stalls as well as at restaurants, and if you go to a Japanese festival you're sure to see and smell it.

Available in cheap Chinese restaurants:

Gyoza	Minced pork and vegetables flavoured with garlic in a pastry case. Eaten with a soy sauce and vinegar dip.

Donburi

Eaten at soba-ya and cheap Japanese and Chinese restaurants, *donburi* means large bowl. The dish is a large bowl heaped with rice and served with something tasty on top. It is inexpensive and available at a large range of restaurants. Americans often call it a rice bowl.

Takuwan	Donburi is most commonly served with a small dish of pickled radishes, yellow in colour and called *takuwan*. They should be eaten last to cleanse the palate.
Katsu-don	The most popular donburi by far – pork fillet, breaded, deep fried, cut into pieces and served with an egg mix on rice.
Ten-don	Two deep fried shrimps (shrimp tempura) on rice.
Oyako-don	Pieces of chicken with egg and onion on rice.
Gyū don	*Sukiyaki*-style beef on rice.
Una-don	Baked eel on rice – the Japanese believe that eel gives the body energy, and eat it especially in the summer. Usually sold at specialist *unagi-ya* (eel shops).
Chuka-don	A Chinese dish. The rice is served with vegetables (such as bamboo, carrot, onion), a few slices of pork and a quail's egg. Available at cheap Chinese restaurants and some soba-ya.
Other rice dishes *Chā-han*	A Chinese dish – fried rice with a mixture of meats or egg and vegetables. Sold in cheap Chinese restaurants and soba-ya.
Hayashi raisu	Beef, onion and gravy with rice. Also served in cheap Chinese restaurants and in soba-ya.
Onigiri also *omusubi* or *nigirimeshi*	A cold dish – small round balls of cooked, cold rice, wrapped around with *nori* (dried seaweed) and with a tasty centre filling, for example, *umeboshi* (pickled plum), *tarako* (cooked cod roe). Eaten at special restaurants called *ochazuke-ya*,

お品書き

うどん

か け	300円
きつね	450円
たぬき	450円
月 見	500円
てんぷら	650円
おかめ	600円
なべやき	800円

そば

も り	300円
ざ る	350円
か け	300円
きつね	450円
たぬき	450円
月 見	500円
てんぷら	650円
おかめ	600円

どんぶり

親子丼	600円
かつ丼	700円
天 丼	800円
チャーシューメン	500円
やきそば	450円
カレーライス	450円

MENU

Udon

kake	¥300
kitsune	¥450
tanuki	¥450
tsukimi	¥500
tempura	¥650
okame	¥600
nabe-yaki	¥800

Soba

mori	¥300
zaru	¥350
kake	¥300
kitsune	¥450
tanuki	¥450
tsukimi	¥500
tempura	¥650
okame	¥600

Donburi

oyako-don	¥600
katsu-don	¥700
ten-don	¥800
cha-shu-men	¥500
yaki soba	¥450
kare raisu	¥450

A typical menu for a small noodle shop. The version on the right in roman letters would rarely appear, so it is a good idea to learn the names of a few dishes before venturing out.

© Hiroshi Umemura 1985

and often bought as a take-away, *onigiri* are also an indispensable part of a Japanese picnic.

Bentoo   Rectangular boxes (wood or plastic) with compartments for different foods, and the name for a cheap set dinner.

Chicken *bentoo*	Fried chicken, salad and rice. A very popular dish served in a wide range of restaurants.
Maku-no-uchi	Sashimi, tempura, pickles, etc. and rice sprinkled with sesame seeds. Available in traditional Japanese restaurants and in department stores.
Ekiben	Bentoo served on stations and trains, and sometimes reflecting the specialities of the region.

Tempura   Brought to Japan in the seventeenth century by the Portuguese, *tempura* is a deep fried food such as shrimp, prawn, squid, eggplant, pepper, onion or sweet potato.

The best tempura is served at a tempura shop, *tempura-ya*, where the oil is changed for each frying (and afterwards sold to lower-class restaurants).

tempura teishoku	Tempura with rice – like a bentoo and inexpensive. Particularly good at a department store restaurant where there is usually a range of *tempura teishoku*, costing, for example, ¥1,000, ¥1,500 or ¥2,000. Usually, served with a side dish of sashimi.

Tonkatsu   Sold at special *tonkatsu* shops and much cheaper than tempura (at, say, ¥1,000 per person), *tonkatsu* is a deep-fried pork cutlet cut up and served with grated cabbage, rice and miso soup. It is eaten with a dip made from Worcester sauce and mustard. It is best to go to a specialist tonkatsu shop *tonkatsuya* for this dish.

In tonkatsuya, a popular alternative order is deep fried breaded shrimps – *ebi furai*. These are eaten with the same Worcester sauce dip, or with tartare sauce. Hanbaga are also available at tonkatsu shops.

Yakitori

Made from chicken (perhaps chicken liver pieces), and various vegetables (for example, leeks), broiled on a bamboo skewer, a *yakitori* is similar to a kebab. It must be accompanied by beer or *sake*, Japan's most celebrated alcoholic beverage (see p.58); *yakitoriya* (yakitori shops) are smoky, roisterous affairs – standard places for businessmen to wind down (and generally inexpensive).

Sushi and sashimi

The cost of *sushi* and *sashimi* varies with the cost of fish, but it is usually expensive. In fact these are the two most celebrated and expensive dishes in Japan. Only the finest fish is used and presentation is of the essence. Sushi is made with a lightly flavoured rice (adding vinegar, salt and sugar) and raw fish. Sashimi is thinly sliced raw fish.

Sushi shops (*sushiya*) are quite an institution in Japan. The cheapest have a moving conveyor belt, from which customers select several dishes, all sold at a standard price. Sushi is a popular take-away, and either Japanese soup, tea, beer or sake is drunk with it. Sushi à la carte is extremely expensive and it is more economical to follow a set menu.

		Sushi selections
Nigiri-zushi	This literally means rice and thin raw fish, and *nigiri zushi* is a dozen or so pieces of sushi including shrimp, tuna and abalone served on a wooden platter.	
Chirashi zushi	A bowl of (cold) rice covered in marinated fish.	
Maki	These must be ordered individually. Try *futo-maki*, rolls of rice and vegetables wrapped in nori; or *kappa-maki*, with cucumber and horse-radish in the centre.	

Inari-zushi	Rice in a case made of fried tofu – it has a fairly sweet taste.
Sashimi teishoku	A selection of sashimi with rice, soup and usually some kind of vegetable.
Chawan-mushi	Sold at sushi shops and traditional Japanese restaurants, *chawan mushi* is light egg custard served hot and as a side dish with chicken, for example, or shrimps.

Dishes cooked at the table

Cooking food at the table encourages a cosy, friendly atmosphere. These occasions are particularly good for a get-together. Except for the last, the following dishes prepared in this way are expensive and are to be eaten only in rather specialized restaurants:

Shabu-shabu	*Shabu-shabu* is the sound of something swept through water. In a large pot of boiling water in the centre of the table you cook your own food from a giant selection of sliced beef, Chinese cabbage, leeks, tofu, etc. There is a miso dip for the beef.
Sukiyaki	Beef (or very occasionally chicken) with vegetables, which you cook in an iron pot at the table in a stock made from sake, sugar, soy sauce and stock (*dashi*). The dip is usually raw egg.
Teppan-yaki	This is cooked for you by your own chef. He cooks a small amount of beef, shellfish and various vegetables at a time on a grill.
Okonomi-yaki	Much cheaper than any of the above, *okonomi-yaki* are thick pancakes containing meat, fish, etc. You cook your own okonomi yaki at your table (turning them over with a spatula). Like *yaki soba*, they are also invariably on sale at festivals.

. . . and Drinking

Soft drinks are available in Japan in all the places you would expect to find them – department stores, restaurants, bars, hotels and so on. *Kissaten* or coffee shops attempt to create their own individual atmosphere with music and decorations, and here you never know what to expect. Coffee is the principal drink on sale, however, along with various other drinks and some food (toast, sandwiches and cakes and perhaps several hot dishes). You may be offered a 'cake set' (a cup of coffee or tea and a cake at a special price). No cup of coffee is cheap, but you may sit in a *kissaten* for as long as you like. The list below gives some of the soft drinks that you will find on menus throughout the country:

Coffee	Young people have taken to calling *kōhi* (alias coffee) *hotto* (i.e. hot coffee). The mildest coffee is referred to as American coffee. The house coffee is called *burendo* (blend) and is always a good bet. Other kinds include *kurimu kōhī* which comes with whipped cream and *aisu kōhī* (iced coffee) which makes a refreshing drink in summer.
Tea	Japanese tea or green tea is called *o cha*. The word for Indian tea is *kocha*. O cha is made with water off the boil and this practice has extended to kocha making. For tea with milk ask for *miruku* tea.
Milk	Milk or *miruku* is either iced or served hot. At stands cartons of milk are known as *gyūnyū shiro*. *Miruku sēki* or a milk shake is also available in Japan and has egg added.

Cocoa	*Kokoa* or cocoa is a strong, tasty drink served with cream on top.
Coca-Cola	Known as *Kōra*.
Float	A *furōto* (float) is the name for any cold drink topped with a scoop of vanilla ice cream.
Cream soda	*Kurīmu soda* or cream soda is a brillant green soda with ice-cream on top.
Orange juice	For real orange juice go to a supermarket; in coffee shops and restaurants you invariably find only *orenji jūsu*, which is carbonated orange, or *orenji huantā* (Fanta), a popular, fizzy brand.

Alcohol There are few restrictions on buying alcohol in Japan. It is on sale at restaurants throughout the day. There are liquor shops everywhere and vending machines which dispense beer, whisky and sake. The Japanese tend not to drink at lunchtime, since they find it rather affects their work in the afternoon! But they make up for their abstinence in the evening. Japan is a country where drinking is tolerated and smiled on. Perhaps it is seen as a good way of relaxing in a society where the individual is regularly under heavy pressure. It is standard procedure for office chums, business associates, etc. to have a drink together. If you are a non-drinker and are invited along for a drink in the bar, it is quite all right to stick to orange juice, but it is vital not to destroy the 'group spirit', which is all important in Japan.

And just in case you should wonder: Japanese women *do* drink, so it is quite in order for western women to accept and enjoy a drink before, during and/or after a meal.

One further tip: if you would like to offer or repay hospitality, it is best to pay for a complete round of drinks rather than to suggest sharing the honour.

Where to drink Take care: some places are very expensive. A shabby exterior does not guarantee reasonable prices. Bar girls always mean high-priced drinks.

Restaurants serving alcohol often put a beer bottle or wine bottle or glass in their sample case. Most restaurants in Japan serve drinks and in some places, like *sushi* or *yakitori* shops, you are expected to drink some alcohol.

Bars open about midday and close around midnight – *nomiya* (cheap bars) in the early hours of the morning. Public transport stops running around midnight, so presumably late revellers have to take taxis home or crash out at a hotel! The following is a brief guide to some of the bars in Japan:

Hotel bars	Bars in hotels list prices on a menu.
Company bars	The big liquor companies – Suntory and Nikka, for example – run bars with standard prices for drinks throughout Japan.
Hostess/cabaret bars	Western and expensive.
Nomiya	These are inexpensive bars where you can sit at the bar on a stool or sit on tatami and eat as well as drink.
Aka-chōchin (one type of nomiya)	*Aka-chōchin* is the red lantern that hangs outside cheap neighbourhood bars, which accordingly have adopted the name. They are also distinguished by a *nawa noren* (rope curtain) hanging at the door.
Beer halls	German-style beer halls with long tables and benches are very popular. They tend to serve dishes of sausages, potatoes and other Germanic fare, and are inexpensive and popular with young people. Similar cheap drinking-places open on the roofs of department stores in the summer.
Karaoke bars	*Karaoke* is live singing to a pre-recorded accompaniment (*kara*

means empty and *oke* is an abbreviation of the word 'orchestra'). At karaoke bars you can both listen to this music and have a turn at the microphone and join in. Karaoke songs are usually lyrical and sentimental.

What to drink   *Beer* is always served chilled, in bottles (or draught, in summer especially), rather like lager. The four big breweries are: Kirin, Sapporo, Asahi and Suntory, and when you get to know what you like, you order by name. Some restaurants serve a *jokki* or *pitchaa* (pitcher), a big jug of beer enough for a group. The word *jokki* also means a beer mug and is commonly used when ordering draught beer.

Whisky. Japanese whisky is much cheaper than imported brands. Suntory and Nikka dominate the market and undoubtedly make the cleverest TV advertisements. The Japanese like to drink whisky with a lot of ice.

Wine. Many European and Californian wines are available in Japanese supermarkets. Prices start at about ¥1,500 a bottle. The Japanese have their own wines which are reasonable. The biggest bottler is Suntory.

Spirits. Western spirits (brandy, gin and vodka) are readily available in Japan and there are also good Japanese brands of all these spirits, at much lower prices. Western liqueurs (for example, creme de menthe) are increasingly popular, though they tend to form the basis of a cocktail rather than being a drink after dinner.

Sake or *seishu* or *nihonshu* is the distinctive drink of Japan. Sake is the everyday word for the drink, but it can also refer to alcoholic drinks in general. Seishu or nihonshu are the more formal terms, and little used when ordering. It is made from rice and is about 17 per cent alcohol. It is drunk in the same year that it is made, since it does not improve with age and there are no vintage years. You can see huge sake barrels outside bars and as offerings at shrines and temples. It plays a part in many traditional Japanese ceremonies –

a bride and groom, for example, always exchange cups of sake.

Sake is usually served hot. It is put in flasks (*tokkuri*), and poured from these into tiny cups (*sakazuki*) or less frequently into small wooden boxes. The cup is usually emptied at a gulp and must be speedily refilled, keeping a keen eye on the cups of friends around you.

Shō-chū is 24–45 per cent proof and is made from rice, sweet potatoes or soba. In the past it has had a rather poor image, but is now breaking into fashionable circles. It is said that shō-chū does not leave you with a hangover, but this, frankly, is a Japanese myth. *Chū-hai* – made from shō-chū – is currently having a major effect on beer sales.

Ume-shu or plum wine is made from Japanese plums, shō-chū and sugar. It is delicious and somewhat like a liqueur. Many Japanese have persuaded themselves that ume-shu is a pick-me-up.

Etiquette

Don't start drinking until everyone's glass is full and the leader has said 'Kampai' (Cheers) and has perhaps made a little speech and everyone has clinked glasses.

It is polite to pour out other people's drinks and not to fill up your own glass. By convention, women pour for men, juniors for seniors and hosts for guests. It is good manners to lift your glass or cup upwards towards the pourer as they serve you.

It is very common to switch from one drink to another in the course of the evening. For example, at a banquet, a glass of wine or champagne, beer to toast the event may be followed by whisky, beer and sake. Sometimes you may have several different drinks on the go at once.

A lot of drinking usually leads to a sing-song; as a businessman, if you can sing a song in English, you may well land your company a fat contract.

Nibbles to accompany drinks

It is not usual to drink without having some small side dish to dip into. As well as nuts, crisps (chips in Japan) and cheese, one might encounter:

natto	fermented soy beans in a sticky paste
sansai nitsuke	broiled fern, which sounds odd, but is delicious
yasai nitsuke	a cooked vegetable mix
oden	vegetables, kamaboko, eggs, daikon (you either love it or hate it!)
yudōhu	boiled tofu with ginger and spring onions and soy sauce. (The yudōhu at Nanzenji Temple, Kyoto, is famous throughout Japan.)

Shopping

Shopping is a delight in Japan. Service is excellent, goods are always neatly wrapped, there is enormous variety, and no bargaining. Alas, the yen is a bit too strong for most tourists, but you can always look.

Opening hours

department stores	10 am – 6 or 6.30 pm
small shops	9 or 10 am – 8 pm or later

Shops open on Saturdays and Sundays, though there is a day when they are closed in the middle of the week, usually Wednesday or Thursday.

The best place to look for shops (and restaurants) is in and around stations. Notice the street decorations: branches of artificial foliage overhead, which change with the seasons.

Some words and phrases

Shopkeepers and restaurateurs use the same patter with customers:

irrashaimase	Welcome, thank you for coming to my shop, etc.

Some of the following phrases may prove useful:

(kore wa) ikura desuka?	how much (is this)?
kore o kudasai	this please
kekko desu	that's all right (when you are looking round, but a salesperson insists on giving you his or her undivided attention).

Department stores

The big chain stores are a mighty institution in Japan (Daimaru, Hankyu, Isetan, Tokyu, Takashimaya, Seibu, Sogo, Matsuzakaya, Mitsukoshi – the list is endless). In these stores service reaches its apogee. Watch out for staff welcoming you at the entrance, on to the escalator and into the lift.

The Japanese department store has always striven for something more than glamour, however. On the upper floors you will often find an art gallery and a concert hall, sometimes there are educational facilities too. People may say, 'I learn French at Tokyu', which is like saying 'I learn French at Selfridges'.

Department-store shopping is convenient and easy, and there is usually a world-wide shipping service. A store guide in English is often available at the information desk. Stores have a large range of restaurants and first-class washrooms.

Supermarkets   Japanese supermarkets are remarkably similar to western ones, and are stocked with as many different products – the more expensive (meat, dairy products, cheese, tea); the moderately priced (fruits, vegetables, bread, coffee); and the cheap (bananas, oranges, *tofu*). Japanese people like chicken and beef and some pork, but they rarely eat lamb. The Japanese market is now flooded with meat from Australia and the US. Familiar cuts are found in a supermarket, but there are many strange packs of very thinly sliced beef – these are used for sukiyaki, teppan-yaki, Japanese barbecue, etc. (see p.54). It is unusual to find large pieces of meat for roasting.

There is a fantastic range of fresh fish in Japan and fish may take up as much room in a supermarket as meat. Many of the fish sold are unfamiliar to westerners, but there is cod (which can be rather salty), and there is also salmon which is first class in Japan (salted salmon less expensive, smoked salmon more expensive).

Frozen foods are plentiful. At the same time, supermarkets generally have a hot counter at which you can buy *tempura*, rice and so on.

Fruit and vegetables are worth a mention as they are so good in Japan; don't forget that the climate throughout the country is extremely varied and that the semi-tropical zones are on Japan's doorstep.

Mikan or Japanese oranges (we call them satsumas

– in fact, a place in Kyushu) are small, sweet and very cheap. You can buy them by the kilo. I once travelled on a train of orange pickers through southern Japan - we ate oranges and drank sake all the way! Mikan are at their best in December. Some other fruits and vegetables are as follows:

nashi	half pear/half apple available in autumn only
kaki	persimmon (autumn only)
pineapple	available throughout the year (from Taiwan, Malaysia), you can buy them whole or sliced
beans and peas	usually sold ready shelled
daikon	a long radish
naganegi	Japanese leeks
bananas	(extremely cheap)
shiitake	enormous dried mushrooms
gobo	long root
renkon	lotus roots
takenoko	fresh bamboo
tofu (bean curd)	particularly good in Japan.

Of course there are also all the more familiar fresh vegetables like cabbages, carrots, beans, etc.

Fruit and vegetable markets

There are fruit and vegetable markets in Japan, but not many. Be careful: you will not be permitted to handle delicate produce before you buy it.

Pharmacies

Pharmacies with a large stock of imported medicines and toiletries are:

American Pharmacy, Yurakucho, Tokyo
Hibiya Pharmacy, Yurakucho
Fuji Pharmacy, Otemachi, Tokyo
Sasanami Pharmacy, Kyoto
Shin-Asahi Pharmacy, Osaka

Shopping for pleasure
Luxuries

A wide variety of chocolates, drink, cigars, tobacco and cigarettes is available in shops and department stores everywhere.

Imported foods

If you crave imported foods, you will find a good selection at two Tokyo stores: the Kinokuniya in

Aoyama, and the Meidiya in Hiroo. But you will also find many familiar western brands of food on ordinary supermarket shelves.

Flowers   Flowers are usually on sale at stands near railway stations. Flower shops and stalls offer a wonderful service – bargain bunches of flowers and a large variety of more expensive flowers wrapped beautifully for you, with a selection of ribbons of different colours to choose from.

Books   The biggest importers of foreign books are:

> Kinokuniya, Shinjuki, Tokyo
> Maruzen, Nihonbashi, Tokyo
> Maruzen, Kyoto

Prices are obviously much higher than in Britain and America so that books make very good presents. Popular (especially controversial) western books are invariably translated into Japanese.

Cameras,   Some people think Hong Kong and Singapore sell
watches,   Japanese goods at a lower price than in Japan. If
electrical   shopping in Japan, look either for a price where the
goods   sales tax (5–50 per cent) is deductible (the shop will put a slip in your passport), or look for a good price (about 30 per cent below the usual price) which takes account of a possible sales tax deduction.

For good-value cameras and watches go to the Shinjuku area of Tokyo (seek out the Yodobashi Camera Co., the Doi Camera Co., or Sakuraya). For electrical goods, the Akihabara district of Tokyo offers the largest selection and the best prices.

Pearls and   The best and most expensive store for precious stones
other precious   is Mikimoto, which has branches throughout Japan,
stones   including Toba, where in 1905 Kokichi Mikimoto cultivated the first spherical pearl.

But shop around for pearls. Investigate several stores before buying. You will also see many fine examples of cloisonné, damascene and coral. Coral, however, is becoming more and more rare.

Japan produces excellent quality cotton and fabulous silk (although the silk industry is now in decline). Among the traditional clothes of interest to the foreign buyer are the *yukata*, the *happi* coat and the *kimono*.

Japanese specialities
Fabrics and clothes

The yukata makes a nice summer dressing-gown. The happi coat (originally a jacket worn by servants or retainers and emblazoned with their master's emblem) goes well with jeans as something different. A kimono is a kimono! It is both expensive and difficult to put on, though the Japanese say it is good for western women as they have the fuller figure suitable for its design. (Be warned, however, that the Japanese really think westerners look rather odd in Japanese clothing!) With the kimono and sometimes with the yukata you should wear an *obi*, a silk band like a belt. You may be able to get a second-hand kimono quite cheaply, and this would do as a souvenir. Try the Oriental Bazaar in Omote Sando, Tokyo. Specifically tourist shops (in the International Arcade near the Imperial Hotel, Tokyo, for example) have yukata and kimono which take account of the longer arms and legs of foreign visitors.

The Japanese also produce an extensive range of beautiful ceramics. Department stores generally offer a good choice, but if you see a particular piece that you like, you should buy it, as it may only be available in that region. Some famous names are:

Pottery and porcelain

Arita, Imari, Satsuma and Karatsu (Kyushu)
Kutani (Ishikawa Prefecture)
Kiyomizu (Kyoto)
Hagi (Yamaguchi Prefecture)
Bizen (Okayama Prefecture)
Mashiko (Tochigi Prefecture)
Seto and Tokoname (Aichi Prefecture)

Okura and Noritake are modern companies; Noritake House is in Tokyo. (Note that a set of cups and saucers or bowls traditionally numbers five and not six, as in the West.)

Ceramic work has always been considered a great art form in Japan and a number of aristocrats became potters in the sixteenth century. One of the great prizes in the wars with Korea in this period were potters who were brought back to Japan and kept in luxurious captivity. The Japanese have always acknowledged the influence of Korean pottery on their own.

The Europeans who saw Japanese ceramics in the sixteenth century were delighted with them, but only one part of the tradition interested them – that which was colourful and decorated. Simple Japanese pottery which was at least as highly regarded by the Japanese did not interest the Renaissance travellers. The Japanese have always admired the plain and simple – even the odd – and all the pottery used in the tea ceremony and in *ikebana* (flower arranging) is of this kind. It was not until this century and the visits of Bernard Leech, the British potter, to Japan that the other side of Japanese taste became known to the West.

In the nineteenth century the Japanese began to make pottery exclusively for export. This was highly decorated and today often appears rather unappealing to the western eye.

Swords Japan at one time produced the finest swords in the world (the *katana* was the symbol of the samurai class, see p.106) and many foreigners still go to Japan to buy swords. The Japan Sword Company, a famous swordsmith, can be found at 3–8–1 Toranomon, Minato-ku, Tokyo (tel. 434–4321). If you live in Japan, ownership of swords (or guns) must be registered with the police.

Lacquer ware Japan has superb lacquer ware. Lacquer is made by applying twenty layers of sap from the lacquer tree mixed with oil to a wood base. Each layer has to be left several days to dry. Real lacquer (*urushi*) is very expensive, though it will last for centuries. It is light in weight, usually black, brown or dark red in colour, and can be cleaned with no more than a damp sponge. If your purse will not stretch to real lacquer, there are now excellent plastic imitations, which bring this traditional art form within everyone's reach. Besides beautiful bowls and trays, you may see lacquer *jubako*, tiered boxes once used for aristocratic picnics – each drawer containing a different food.

Kanazawa (Wajima), Aizu, Shunkei and Tsugaru are famous for their lacquer ware.

Netsuke are small carvings usually in ivory. They were made in the Edo period (1603–1868) and were used as decorations or as good luck charms. It was particularly common to fasten them to kimonos. Netsuke frequently represented plants or animals (for example, the Zodiac animals), and are now avidly sought by collectors. *Netsuke*

Ivory is cheaper in Singapore and Hong Kong than in Japan, and the Japanese rarely use ivory except perhaps for their *hanko* or *inkan* (personal seals), with which they sign all letters and documents.

Kokeshi
© Hiroshi Umemura 1985

Dolls make fine presents. There are two kinds: *Dolls*

kokeshi	cylindrical wooden dolls from rural areas which are fairly inexpensive
ningyo	the traditional life-like dolls that the Japanese display in their homes in glass cases; these are expensive (department stores will ship them for you, together with the case).

Other traditional arts and crafts Look out too for woodblock prints (originals and reproductions); paper goods (try Kyukyodō and Hoya stores on the Ginza, Tokyo); fans (visit Miyawaki Baisen and Co. in Kyoto); and *kakejiku* or hanging scrolls.

Symbols Certain recurrent motifs run throughout the traditional art and craftwork of Japan. Some of the more common are as follows:

the crane	a bird that symbolizes good fortune and inhabits some parts of Japan (it is the symbol of Japan Airlines)
the tortoise	also a symbol of long life and good fortune
the carp	a fish that symbolizes boyhood, energy, vigour, determination
bamboo	a plant able to withstand cold winters and thus a symbol of frankness, strength and warmth of heart
the *ume*	plum
the *sakura*	cherry
the *kiku*	chrysanthemum (the imperial flower).

Leisure, pleasure and sport

The Japanese perform western classic music excellently and provide superb facilities for its enjoyment. A famed venue is the Tokyo Metropolitan Festival Hall (tel. 828–2111) which is part of the culture complex at Ueno.

Concerts
Western classical music

You can buy tickets for concerts at department stores or at the concert hall itself, but your hotel will be able to book for you. Large companies buy up blocks of seats for the best series of concerts; as a visitor you may find that you are offered a couple of these seats.

Pop concerts given by Japanese or western groups are held regularly, but admission is expensive.

Pop concerts

The disco areas of Tokyo are Shinjuku, Shibuya and Roppongi. The price of admission for boys is sometimes higher than that for girls. Discos play mostly western music and some Japanese pop.

Discos

There is every chance that you will see the same films showing in Tokyo as in London, Sydney or New York. Foreign films have subtitles and are not dubbed in Japan. Tokyo and other cities abound in cheap cinemas showing old films, organizing 'seasons' and so on. The best lists appear in the *Tokyo Journal* and *Kansai Time Out*.

Movies

There are generally three or four performances of each film every day – one in the morning, one in the afternoon and one or two in the evening. A cinema ticket costs ¥1,500–¥2,000 in the smarter theatres, though there are reductions for students. At the cheaper theatres tickets may be half this price. Your ticket will usually be for an unnumbered seat. (Tips are *never* offered or expected.)

Television   There are seven TV channels in the Tokyo area, two of which are NHK (government-controlled) and have a rather public-service feel to them. NHK channels broadcast more educational, documentary and news programmes and show more classical drama and music than the other channels, which are private and rely on revenue from commercials.

The Japanese like to watch baseball games (every evening in the season) and some wrestling. In the winter there is rugby at weekends – there is a varsity league with competition between such prestigious universities as Keio and Waseda (dubbed the Oxford and Cambridge of Japan). Soccer which is rapidly growing in popularity is also shown on TV.

The Japanese are very keen on watching dramatic productions, many of which are historical and are sometimes called samurai dramas. The plots always follow a similar pattern.

There are also many quiz programmes, soap operas and cookery programmes, and several language programmes: from 6 to 8 am, 7 to 7.30 pm and 11 to 11.30 pm each day. There are programmes to learn English, French, German and Chinese and a large number of people follow these. However, the Japanese remain very bad at speaking other people's languages, and *foreign programmes* are dubbed.

Even if you can't understand the Japanese language, watching TV can tell you a lot about the country. For example, there are the commercials showing the Japanese desire for California-style homes. There is the sumo wrestling shown continuously when there is a tournament. There is the love of history and tradition (samurai drama). There are countless travel programmes (the Japanese love to travel). Some programmes are considerably more violent than in the west and several late night pornographic shows would certainly not be broadcast either in Britain or America. Chat shows look fascinating; you only wish you could understand it all!

Anyone who begins to get the slightest feel for Japan and its people will find the TV fascinating. I recommend the column 'Nothing Highbrow' in the

Evening Asahi on Mondays, which gives a background to the showbiz TV world in Japan. There is also a little known but excellent magazine *Eye ai*, which every month prints all the gossip and news about Japanese TV and film celebrities, as well as other interesting articles on Japan. It has wide sales among the Japanese abroad (for example, in Hawaii and California).

A large number of foreign programmes are shown on Japanese TV, but, as we have said, they are almost without exception dubbed into Japanese. (Even a speech by the British Queen was dubbed on her visit to Japan, but this was quickly reversed after huge outcries from the Japanese who demanded to hear *the* authentic Queen's English. Records of the Queen's speeches have been bestsellers in Japan!) However, the BBC Shakespeare series has escaped dubbing.

If you acquire a multiplex adapter you can get the news and perhaps a film in English every day on one or other of the different channels (there is the odd film in another language). These programmes are termed 'bi-lingual' and are listed as such in the English newspapers. (There are 'bi-lingual' broadcasts on all channels from time to time.) Some hotels and apartment blocks have cable TV with continuous (American) television.

Radio

| Classical music: | NHK FM (82.5 MHz Tokyo area, a Japanese service) |
| Pop: | FEN: the Far East Network (of the American services), AM 810 KHz, which broadcasts 24 hours a day for American servicemen and women and millions of other listeners. |

Bathing

The Japanese have always liked bathing. There are numerous hot springs (*onsen*) which make it convenient and practical, and the Shinto religion, with its emphasis on purification, has doubtless added encouragement.

Onsen have become real resorts with hotels and

restaurants, but the gatherings at Japanese spas have never been as class conscious as those in Europe. Some of the most famous are in Kyushu. All Japanese like an onsen holiday, and you too may enjoy a prolonged soak.

Every neighbourhood also has its bath house or *huroya/sento* (often with laundries attached to utilize the hot water). But take a friend along with you to show you the ropes.

There are the *Koshitsu yokujo* which are like Turkish baths in the West. They are expensive and in areas like Kabukicho (Shinjuku, Tokyo) highly sensual.

Geisha One senses that the Japanese are rather fed up with foreigners' questions about geisha. The answers are always too pat: 'The geisha is a centuries-old professional entertainer.' Trained geisha are only found in Tokyo and Kyoto (for example, in Akasaka and Shimbashi in Tokyo, and in Gion in Kyoto) and a few places outside (most notably at onsen). The true geisha has to be able to orchestrate an evening superbly and be the soul of discretion afterwards. But women who have not received a geisha training also dress as geisha and offer some of the same services at restaurants and hotels.

Entertainment with geisha is an honour accorded to visiting businessmen. If you have to pay for a taste of geishadom yourself, it will be very expensive.

Background Geisha literally means an art person or persons, and accordingly a geisha has always been expected to be accomplished in the arts – traditional singing, dancing and playing the *shamisen* (see p.80). Additionally, the geisha has to be able to converse and create the right atmosphere for her clients. The geisha has in Japan helped to fill the role of the sophisticated hostess in the West, making things go well at dinners and functions, and today you may well encounter geisha in that capacity.

Of course, geisha, often beautiful and alluring, have gone beyond this role. As early as the 1700s when geisha first appeared in Japan, the government passed regulations attempting to forbid the geisha from taking work from their first employers – the courtesans of Kyoto and Tokyo.

Geisha offer one of the few long-term jobs for women in Japan, for a woman can remain a geisha until she takes other work or marries. Ex-geisha often run successful restaurants and bars of their own. Geisha have sometimes married their customers, though more usually the geisha have been their mistresses. Indeed, until the last war geisha had to have a patron (*danna*), and he was often selected for them by the geisha house. The geisha world or 'flower and willow world' (Karyūkai) is carefully regulated. A geisha must undertake a lengthy apprenticeship and take a qualifying exam! She belongs to a geisha house (*okiya*) which in turn belongs to a group (*hanamachi*) in a given area. Its registry office (*kemban*) handles all bookings, schedules and fees. Bookings come from hotels and night clubs, but above all from *ryotei* – high class traditional restaurants. A customer pays for a meal and the services of geisha on the same bill (which is taxed). The kemban gives the geisha her fee, but additionally, she receives a substantial tip from her customers! It is unlikely to find geisha working for below ¥25,000 for two hours.

The profession

There are geisha in Tokyo, Kyoto and the onsen or hot spring resorts (though the geisha in Tokyo and Kyoto are considered to be in a class of their own). The geisha areas in Tokyo are Shimbashi and Akasaka, and the hanamachi in Akasaka are famous for their connection with government politicians. The famous geisha areas of Kyoto are Gion and Pontocho. A visitor to Japan might want to see a geisha as, dressed in elaborate kimono and beautifully coiffured, they make their way to appointments in the evening. Hotels might help a foreigner make a 'geisha booking', but it is an area where one needs contacts and know-how (and money!). If, as a visiting businessman, you are offered a night in the 'flower and willow world', you are being greatly honoured.

Location

There will be lively conversation (perhaps for the occasion an English-speaking geisha will be found) and elaborate entertainments. It will certainly be something to remember.

Bar girls/ hostesses Some bars in the entertainment districts of big cities have bar girls or hostesses. They join your table and help with the entertainment. They are not trained like the geisha and usually wear western dress and not kimono. Many Japanese find that they are able to relax more readily in the hostesses' company than in that of geisha, though there can be no comparison in the status of the two groups in Japanese society. A bar with hostesses will be vastly more expensive than an ordinary bar, and if it is just a drink you want, you should steer clear.

Masseurs/ masseuses There are many quite legitimate masseurs and masseuses in Japan, but those operating in toruko buro (Turkish baths) in entertainment districts like Kabuki-cho in Tokyo's Shinjuku also cater to their customers' sensual demands. There have been protests recently in the Turkish press that a Turkish bath in Japan really means no such thing!

Traditional sports
Sumo Sumo is Japanese-style wrestling. Wrestlers weigh between 125 and 175 kilogrammes and maintain their figure by eating a huge meal each evening before going to bed. Their weight is concentrated in the stomach and hips, and the principle of sumo is one of pushing (and being pushed). If a wrestler is pushed out of the ring, or if any part of his body (except his feet) touches the floor, he has lost.

Devotees of the sport include the Emperor, and it is not easy to get seats. If you do, you will probably end up at the newly built Kokugikan Sumo Hall (tel. 821–2201).

The martial arts The martial arts developed from the martial skills employed by the samurai warrior class in battle (see p.106) and the spiritual training which became increasingly important to them. With the abolition of the samurai class after the Meiji Restoration (1868), it became possible for anyone to practise these arts, though practitioners tended to belong to exclusive sects which emphasized obedience and the ideal of national self-defence. After the Second World War, the martial arts were popularized as sports which upheld the philosophies of harmony and universality. The appeal of these arts to the west has grown markedly, and many westerners now go to Japan to improve their skills.

Judo – the 'soft way' is popular everywhere, particularly in schools and colleges. For information contact the All-Japan Judo Federation, c/o Kodokan, 1–16–30, Kasuga, Bunkyo-ku, Tokyo (tel. 811–7151).

Kendo (the way of the sword) is Japanese fencing, which these days limits itself to bamboo staves. The idea is to hit three designated parts of your opponent's body (head, trunk, forearm) or to stab his neck. The Japanese championships are held in December. For information contact the Japan Kendo Federation, c/o Nippon Budokan, 2–3, Kitanomaru-Koen, Chiyoda-Ku, Tokyo (tel. 221–5804/5). The Metropolitan Police Board (tel. 581–4321) gives free instruction.

Aikido (the way of spirit power) combines elements of judo, kendo and karate. For the full story get in touch with the Aikido World Headquarters, 102, Wakamatsucho, Shinjuku-ku, Tokyo (tel. 203–9236).

Kyudo (the way of archery) is the oldest of Japan's martial arts. The bow is long (2.25 metres) and the rules precise. The best display of the old art of *yabusame* – archery on horseback – can be seen at the Hachimangu Shrine, Kamakura in mid-September. The All Japan Kyudo Federation, Kishi Memorial Hall, 4th fl, 1–1–1, Jinnan, Shibuya-ku, Tokyo (tel. 467–7949), has all the necessary information.

Karate is associated with Japan, but, in fact, only reached the mainland of Japan from China via Okinawa after the First World War. Information on courses and demonstrations is available from the World Union of Karate-do Organisation, 4th fl. Senpaku Shinkokai Bldg., 1–15–16, Toranomon, Minato-ku, Tokyo (tel. 503–6637).

Other sports   The Japanese are addicted to baseball. Their two
Baseball   professional leagues – the Central and Pacific – each
with six teams, keep Japan in a fevered state from
April to October. The two big stadiums in Tokyo are
the Korakuen Stadium, 1–3–61, Koraku, Bunkyo-ku,
(tel. 811–2111), and the Jungu Stadium, Meiji Shrine
Outer Garden, 13, Kasumigaoko, Shinjuku-ku, (tel.
402–2115).

Fishing   There is a great deal of fishing in Japan. Popular
fishing spots are lakes Saiko and Motosu near Mount
Fuji and Lake Chuzenji at Nikko. Tokyo and other
cities have specially designated fishing ponds (for
example, Ichigaya in Tokyo).

Some lakes are owned by hotels – guests can
practically fish from the back door! If you are an
enthusiastic angler, a Japanese travel agency will
probably be willing and able to arrange a package for
you (permits, accommodation, etc.)

Fishing permits are needed only in certain places,
where they are issued by the local fishermen's union.

Skiing   Skiing is an increasingly popular sport, and the long
university vacations (from February onwards) seem
designed to allow students to invade the slopes. There
are ski resorts everywhere, but especially in the
Japanese Alps (Chubu) and in Hokkaido.

Golf   It is perhaps as expensive to play golf as to be
entertained by a geisha. A company may treat visiting
overseas businessmen to a day at the golf course.
(Japanese businessmen invariably like the idea of a
golf match when they are in Britain or America.)
Throughout Japanese cities there are public practice
ranges where anyone can practise and knock balls
into nets. (Until you get used to it, it can be rather
alarming to see some ranges perched on the tops of
buildings!)

Swimming   Public swimming pools are clean, well maintained
and regularly inspected by the local health authority.
The best pool in Tokyo is the Olympic Pool near
Meiji Park. It is open to the public all the year round.

© John Weatherhill Inc.

A lot of outdoor public swimming pools close in
September, when for Americans and Europeans it still
feels warm enough to swim. Large hotels often have a
swimming pool, but the rates are high – about ¥1,000
per hour. Publicly owned swimming pools levy rates
at about ¥100–300 per session.

Jogging is practised by millions of people throughout   *Jogging*
Japan. The outer moat of the Imperial Palace is a
particularly popular circuit. In any park early in the
morning you will not only encounter joggers, but all
sorts of healthy activities in full swing. The parks
become so full that jogging becomes the art of skilful
manoeuvre.

The traditional arts

Japanese theatre Japanese theatre is not to everyone's liking, but the plot can be grasped by reading the synopsis in the programme several times before the performance starts – you can sometimes hire headphones and listen to an English commentary. Japanese theatre includes music, dance, beautiful costumes and scenery. The artistic impact is tremendous. Men play all the roles (male and female), and some kabuki actors in particular are great beauties on stage.

A Noh mask
© Hiroshi Umemura 1985

Noh. The theme of *Noh* drama is often tragic. The actors often use distinctive masks, and hand movements are all important. Noh was perfected in the fifteenth century, and was entertainment for the aristocracy. A very old stage has survived at the Itsukushima shrine in Miyajima and is often used for Noh plays.

Kyōgen drama developed alongside Noh. It is humorous and employs a very small cast. Kyōgen works very well (and is mainly performed) as a comic interlude between Noh plays. It has become extremely popular (in Japanese and in translation) with western audiences.

Kabuki. Noh audiences are suitably sombre, but *kabuki*-goers look a different lot and munch bentoo and oranges during the performance, which is going further than any British audience would dare to go! Kabuki grew up in the seventeenth century as an entertainment for the urban middle classes. Plots are heavily historical or based on legend, and the theme is usually the conflict between duty and true love. A good kabuki performance includes dancing, music and some comedy.

Bunraku is traditional Japanese puppetry. Performances are as long as a play, but there may be a selection of scenes from different plays. The puppets are two-thirds the size of a human figure and their facial expressions can be skilfully manipulated.

For details of theatre performances consult the TIC. Theatres in Tokyo for the various kinds of drama are as follows:

for Noh (and sometimes Kyōgen):

The National Noh Theatre, Tokyo	(423–1331)
Ginza Noh Stage, Tokyo	(571–0197)
Kanze Noh Stage, Tokyo	(469–5241)
Kongo Noh Stage, Kyoto	(075–221–3049)

for kabuki:

Kabukiza, Tokyo	(541–3131)
National Theatre, Tokyo	(265–7411)
Minamiza Theatre, Kyoto	(075–561–1155)
Shin Kabukiza Theatre, Osaka	(06–631–2121)

for bunraku:

National Theatre, Tokyo	(265–7411)
Gion Corner, Kyoto	(075–561–1119)
Asahiza Theatre, Osaka	(06–211–6431)
National Bunraku Theatre, Osaka	(06–212–1122)

Television channels 1 and 3 (in the Tokyo area) regularly broadcast dramatic productions.

Music

All traditional theatrical performances have a musical accompaniment. (You can also go to performances of traditional Japanese music, of course.) Some of the instruments that you are likely to see and hear are the following:

Koto
: This is a stringed instrument six feet long. It is plucked to produce perhaps the most characteristic of Japanese sounds. The *koto* arrived in Japan from China in the eleventh century and has always been associated with refinement and high culture.

Shamisen
: By contrast, the *shamisen* is an indigenous instrument that came to the fore in the sixteenth century. It has three strings which are plucked with a plectrum, and is much like the western banjo. It accompanies everything from drinking songs to classical dramatic themes.

Shakuhashi
: This is a long bamboo flute that also came to Japan from China. It is generally heard as an accompaniment to classical drama.

Taiko
: The *taiko* is the great Japanese drum heard at festivals and recitals.

The tea ceremony Ideally *chanoyu* (or *sadō*) or the tea ceremony should be performed in a thatched tea-house in a beautiful

Reproduced by courtesy of *Punch*

part of a Japanese garden. The bitter-tasting tea is not the point of the long ceremony, but rather the discipline and spiritual satisfaction it induces. The tea ladies wear kimonos and sit on the floor, but as a visitor you are not expected to follow suit. Instead, the ceremonies will be carefully explained to you, allowing you to relax and enjoy the occasion. The TIC can give you information on these ceremonies and many hotels arrange chanoyu.

Flower arrangement

Ikebana (flower arranging) was once closely linked to the tea ceremony, a flower arrangement being placed in the tea room to enhance the mood of the occasion. Today, however, arrangements appear everywhere. Large hotels often have some of the best displays.

For information about courses for foreign visitors contact:

Ikebana International
2nd fl. Shufunotomo Bldg. 1–6
Kanda, Surugadai
Chiyoda-ku, Tokyo
(tel. 293–8188)

Bonsai

Bonsai is the artificial dwarfing of trees and plants so that one seems to be looking at a miniature version of the fully grown specimen. It takes years to produce results. Bonsai originated in China and was introduced to Japan during the Kamakura period (1192–1336). It became popular in Japan among noblemen who wished to copy the shape of a particular tree they had seen on their travels. (Sometimes they reproduced an entire landscape which had caught their eye.)

The art of bonsai was refined to a degree far beyond that reached in China and it is extremely popular in Japan today. The Japanese place bonsai outside or inside their homes for decoration – perhaps in the living-room (see p.16).

Large shrines, for example, the Meiji Shrine in Tokyo, have bonsai displays at various times of the year. Real enthusiasts should go to the Bonsai Village in Bonsai-machi, Omiya, Saitama.

Shodō 'the way of writing'

Shodō (calligraphy) is an important art form in Japan as it is in other East Asian countries. Calligraphy originated in China and came to Japan when Japan began to adopt Chinese writing in about the fifth century. It was used not only to write down Chinese characters (*kanji*), but also in the writing of the *kana* scripts as they developed (see *Language, courtesies and pleasantries*). Calligraphy required artistic and poetic skills and was never considered mere copying – a fine calligrapher was thought to have a fine character.

The Japanese calligrapher works quickly with a thick brush (*ōfude*), a thin brush (*kofude*) and Chinese ink (sumi), a compound including the soot of burned wood and oil or fishbone glue.

Travelling around Japan:
the capital and beyond

Japan's four principal islands (Hokkaido, Honshu, **Size**
Shikoku and Kyushu) and 4,000 smaller ones stretch
in an arc for some 2,790 kilometres (the distance from
Vancouver to San Diego). Japan is about one and a
half times as big as the United Kingdom. Interest-
ingly, maps printed in the West put Japan on the
eastern edge of the map, while those in Japan have
Europe at one edge and America at the other.

The most important features of the Japanese land- **Geography**
scape are its mountains which cover over 70 per cent
of the area of the country. As a result, Japanese cities
often have beautiful mountain backdrops, while
urban areas are among the most crowded in the
world. In fact, Japan's 118 million people (Japan has
the seventh largest population in the world) is
jammed into just 18 per cent of the country's land
space. The relatively small area of agricultural land
(15 per cent of Japan's surface) yields half of the
nation's food.

The latitudinal length of Japan means that there is a **Climate**
wide variety of climate. To take an exaggerated
example, it may be snowing in Hokkaido while
people are swimming in the seas off Okinawa. Japan
has four distinct seasons, corresponding to those in
western Europe and North America. In Tokyo one
feels that spring comes one month earlier than in
England and that summer lasts a month longer. What
English people think of as exceptionally good autumn
weather seems to last into December.

From the point of view of weather, the very best
time to visit Japan is in October and November. It is
warm, skies are blue and there is little rain. The
autumn colours are dazzling. Spring has the *sakura* or

cherry blossom, which is breathtaking but lasts only a
few days around the beginning of April. There is rain
in mid-April. May is generally a lovely month with
warm, sunny days and an abundance of flowers.
From mid-June to mid-July there is the *tsuyu* or rainy
season, when the weather is hot and wet. (Several
days of rain alternate with several very warm, dry
days.) The summer is extremely hot and sticky
throughout most of Japan, with temperatures at least
30°C (86°F) in Tokyo throughout August. The winter
is cold from December onwards and temperatures
may fall below freezing. February is the coldest
month, a sharp shock before spring.

Administrative divisions   Japan is divided into large regions and smaller
prefectures. The regions are areas defined by ge-
ography or history, and are as follows: Hokkaido,
Tohoku, Kanto, Chubu, Kansai (or Kinki), Chugoku, Shikoku, Kyushu and the Okinawa Islands.

The prefectures are the official administrative units
of Japan. The word *ken* (meaning 'prefecture') is
added to the names of 43 of the prefectures, for
example, Hiroshima Ken or Nara Ken; special
appendages are added to Tokyo (*to*) and to Kyoto and
Osaka (*fu*). Hokkaido stands on its own (*do* means
'district' or 'prefecture').

Kanto   The region of Kanto is coterminous with the Kanto
plain. It contains Tokyo, which with a population of
11,360,000 makes it one of the world's largest cities.
Tokyo joins up with encircling satellite cities and
with Yokohama, which is Japan's second largest city.
Yokohama is Japan's major port – followed by Kobe
and Fukuoka. Tokyo is the Japanese capital, and since
the country is so highly centralized it is the centre of
decision-making. Tokyo is the nation's banking and
commercial centre, with Osaka an important second.

In Kanto there is a significant concentration of
industry: heavy industry, electrical goods, car manufacturing and shipbuilding.

Tokyo   You should not be put off by Tokyo's size. It is a city
that breaks down into distinct areas, which are

manageable on foot. Although the overriding impression of Tokyo is one of size and speed, it is amazing how many pleasant backwaters and quaint corners survive.

The Imperial Palace occupies a 250-acre site in the centre of Tokyo. Try walking round its moat for the day, calling at places of interest on your way. (The palace itself is closed to visitors, except for 2 days a year when the public are allowed in to greet the emperor.) On the skyline you will see the National Diet building and the roof of the Nippon Budokan Hall. The area around the Budokan is well worth a visit and nearby is the awesome Yasukuni Shrine, which honours those who died on military service.

Yurakucho and Ginza. The Imperial Palace is on the edge of the Yurakucho area, which has a lot of cinemas. (The TIC office is also here.) Shops are plentiful too in Yurakucho, but completely take over in the Ginza district. From Ginza the *Kabukiza* (kabuki theatre) is within walking distance.

Ueno and Asakusa. This area is what people in Tokyo call downtown. It has some of the oldest residential districts in the city. Ueno Station is one of the biggest in Tokyo. Ueno Park next to this covers a huge area, containing in its midst the Tokyo Metropolitan Festival Hall and a number of important museums. Ueno Zoo is one of the best in Japan with an internationally famous panda. (Full information on the opening times of museums, galleries and zoos is available from JNTO offices and included in their guides to places of interest in Japan. It is worth checking opening times; Monday is frequently a closing day for many museums and galleries.)

Travelling by subway from Ueno, you arrive in Asakusa, famous for its temple dedicated to Kannon, the Goddess of Mercy. It is always crowded.

The *Akihabara* district is a mecca for tourists. It is 'Electric City', where visitors can buy any electrical goods (video recorders etc.) at cut prices.

Shinjuku has one of the most confusing stations in the world – complicated by the fact that two department stores and an elaborate shopping complex are built over the lines (with more shops underground). The station alone is worth a visit. Shinjuku is a district with a hoard of shops, including the Kinokuniya Bookstore. It is also the place for cameras and watches. Pleasure-seekers head for an area called Kabuki-cho, which is like London's Soho, but much more extensive. It is packed with entertainment of every variety. The west side of Shinjuku has a large zone of skyscrapers, mostly fairly new and some still under construction. It looks good in the day, but is spectacular at night. Shinjuku Gyoen (Park) is a very pleasant place, spacious and quiet.

Shibuya. The most famous object in Shibuya is Hachiko, the bronze statue of a dog which exhibited exemplary obedience to its master. The area around Hachiko is *the* meeting-place in Shibuya. The area teems with shops and restaurants.

Harajuku. Shibuya leads into Harajuku, a lively area in which you might feel old over twenty. On Sunday afternoons there is usually street dancing adjacent to the Olympic Swimming Pool, and the road is closed for that purpose.

Aoyama. Leading off from Harajuku is a broad street lined with trees called Omote Sando. Its grandeur has prompted some to dub it the Champs Elysées of Tokyo. At the eastern end it meets with another street, Aoyama Dori, celebrated for its coffee shops and the Kinokuniya supermarket.

The Meiji Shrine is close to Harajuku Station. The shrine, which occupies a huge wooded area, is dedicated to the Emperor Meiji, and is without doubt one of the most popular shrines in Japan. The shrine contains a famous iris garden which blooms in May.

Akasaka, Roppongi and the Tokyo Tower. Akasaka (not to be confused with Asakusa) and Roppongi are both fashionable districts and popular with visitors. Near Roppongi is the Tokyo Tower, similar to the Eiffel Tower, and a Tokyo landmark. There are impressive views from the top which is 333 metres high (1,092 feet).

Ikebukuro has a vast number of shops and cinemas. A particularly large collection of shops and exhibition areas (*and* the passport office) is housed in Ikebukuro's vast Sunshine City.

Tokyo Disneyland. According to surveys the Tokyo Disneyland, opened in 1983 and similar in size and quality to those in the US, is the single most important tourist attraction in Japan. Arriving by bus from Narita airport, you can see it against the skyline. Because it is so popular it is best to buy tickets in advance. (There are various tariffs.) A special bus service runs from Tokyo Station to the Disneyland.

Nikko. A trip to Nikko is a very popular outing. It is best to go by the private Tobu railroad, a journey taking 1 hour and 45 minutes from Asakusa Station.

Trips from Tokyo

In Nikko there is the great Toshogu Shrine, built by the Shogun Iemitsu in 1636 and dedicated to his grandfather the first Tokugawa Shogun, Ieyasu (1542–1616). Like most shrines it is constructed mostly of wood and is a stunning complex set on a hillside. The decoration and carving are vivid; the style might be thought of as Japanese baroque.

After exploring the historical sights, there is usually time on a day trip to visit Lake Chuzenji and the Kegon Falls (which have a 90 metre or 316 foot drop). There are buses, and you can take a sightseeing cruise on Lake Chuzenji. For a small group it might be worthwhile hiring a taxi for a round trip, agreeing the fee before setting out.

Kamakura. You can get to Kamakura by the JNR Yokosuka line from Tokyo Station in an hour. Nearby Enoshima can be reached by the Odakyu line from Shinjuku Station.

Kamakura was the seat of the feudal government from 1192. It has a number of outstanding historical sites, and the town itself is extremely pleasant. After being in Tokyo, it is refreshing to walk along Kamakura beach for a breath of sea air.

The most celebrated site in Kamakura is the Kotokuin Temple, which houses the Daibutsu or the Great Buddha. It is smaller than the Buddha at Nara though still 11.4 metres (or 37.4 feet) in height. The Kamakura Daibutsu's expression is noted for its serenity.

The Tsurugaoka Hachimangu Shrine is also very famous. At New Year it is one of the principal places for the Japanese to visit, and in September there are important and unique celebrations of the festival of Yabusame. There is a huge and prominent ginkgo tree by the steps leading up to the shrine. It is said that an assassin hid behind the tree and murdered the Shogun Minamoto Sanetomo in 1219.

Yokohama. One can go to Yokohama either by JNR from Tokyo Station in 30 minutes or by the Tokyu line from Shibuya Station.

Yokohama developed as a port opened to foreign visitors in the nineteenth century. Therefore, many buildings in Yokohama are western in style. The Municipal Museum, housed in the old British Consulate, and the Silk Museum opposite, are worth visiting. On one of the hills overlooking the city is a famous residential area called the Bluff. Motomachi is a fashionable shopping street and further on is Yokohama's Chinatown, one of the best places to eat Chinese food in Japan. Take a taxi (a short ride) to the Sankeien Garden, a scenic Japanese garden with a number of structures of historic interest brought there from all over Japan.

Hakone is 1 hour 32 minutes from Shinjuku Station, Tokyo, by the Odakyu line's 'Romance' car. (So called because many honeymooners have used this train.)

A major attraction of Hakone-Yumoto and the nearby towns, Miyanoshita, Kowakidani and Gora, are the onsen or hot springs, which are used for bathing.

From Hakone-Yumoto one can go by the Hakone Tozan, or funicular railway, to Chokoku-no-Mori Station and to the Hakone Open Air Museum, which has a number of modern sculptures, some very celebrated. From Gora Station near the Museum one can continue by cable car to Togendai Station and take a steamer on Lake Ashi down to Hakone-Machi. Ashi is a particularly beautiful lake, and you can see Mount Fuji reflected in its waters (the famous inverted reflection).

Atami. You can travel to Atami directly from Tokyo Station by JNR. Atami is a seaside town with hot springs and many hotels. It is the gateway to the

Izu Peninsula, which has a lovely coastline, good for swimming and sunbathing. What recommends Atami above many other attractive places is the MOA Museum of Art, built on a spectacular site overlooking the Pacific. It has over 3,000 Japanese paintings, sculptures and other pieces of art, some of which are classified national treasures. (MOA stands for the Mokichi Okada International Association, a group set up to promote the ideals of Mokichi Okada, who founded a new religion this century.)

Tsukuba. The university and town of Tsukuba have been dubbed by some 'Science City', and Tsukuba was host to the International Science Fair March-September 1985. To reach the town take a train from Tokyo's Ueno Station (Joban line).

Kansai Much industrial and commerical strength is also concentrated in the region of Kansai. There are important sites for the heavy industries, shipbuilding, electronics, textile manufacturing and metal working.

The region has more than economic significance; it is extremely important in terms of Japanese history and culture. Nara was the capital of Japan from 710 to 794 and Kyoto was the capital from 794 to 1868. Between them these two cities have one of the most amazing collections of art and architecture in the world.

The claims for leadership are so finely balanced between the regions of Kanto and Kansai that it is not surprising that the two are considered rivals (though it is surprising that the difference should be so noticeable in Japan). The regions have different accents and styles of cooking. Personalities are also supposed to differ: people from Kanto are said to be more open or brash than those from Kansai and to be either more generous or simply spendthrift.

Kyoto You will probably find Kyoto a very easy city to negotiate if you arrive directly from Tokyo. (The Tourist Information Centre is by the station.) There is a simple subway system, and well-meaning people will put you on the right buses. Taking a taxi now and again will not be so expensive, and will save a lot of time.

To see everything you would certainly need more than a day. Kyoto has 400 Shinto shrines, 1650 Buddhist temples and numerous other places of interest! Kyoto is the centre of traditional industries such as silk weaving, ceramics and lacquer ware and stages three of the great festivals of Japan. (*The Aoi Festival*, 15 May; the *Gion Festival*, 16–17 July; the *Jidai Festival*, 22 October). It is not, however, a city that lives on its memories. It is a dynamic and sometimes radical centre, and its university stands equal first with the University of Tokyo.

Kiyomizudera. The Kīyomizu Temple is one of the symbols of Kyoto, and stands in an imposing position on a hillside in the city affording a marvellous view. The spring, after which the temple was named, bubbles up near its base.

Ginkakuji. This was built in the Muromachi Period (1336–1573) for the Ashikaga Shogunate. The pavilion was originally to have been covered with silver foil, but the shogun died before the project was finished. Ginkakuji has a fine and intriguing garden, and nearby is the delightful Philosophers' Walk (so called because Kitaro Nishida, a famous Japanese philosopher, used to walk there).

Sanjusangendo. Dating from 1226, this temple contains over 1,000 bronze images. The overall effect is dazzling.

Kyoto National Museum. Near to Sanjusangendo is the Kyoto National Museum, which, as we would expect, houses a rich collection of paintings, sculptures and other treasures. It is such an easy and pleasant place to wander round, spacious and airy with all items exhibited to the best advantage. It is open from 9 am – 4 pm daily, but closed on Mondays.

The Imperial Palace was the residence of all the Japanese emperors from around 1300 until 1868. However, since the emperor had little power and money when he lived in Kyoto, the shogun's place in Kyoto is much more grand, though the shogun rarely visited the city.

You need to apply for a pass to view the palace compound (just before the 10 am and 1 pm tours).

Nijo Castle built in 1603 is within reasonable

distance of the Imperial Palace. It was the official residence of the Tokugawa Shoguns (1603–1868) on their rare visits to Kyoto. Nijo Castle is noticeably more lavish than the Imperial Palace, symbolizing the greater wealth and power of the Shogunate. The best-known features of the castle are not the paintings or the architecture, but the 'nightingale floors', which squeak warning the guards of the approach of would-be assassins.

Kinkakuji or the Golden Pavilion was originally a pavilion for the Ashikaga Shogun, Yoshimitsu, in the fourteenth century. It derived its name from the gold leaf used in its decoration.

Ryoanji. In the same area as Kinkakuji is the Ryoanji Temple, which has perhaps the most famous rock garden in Japan. There are fifteen stones set in white sand, the shape and pattern of which have given rise to various interpretations through the ages.

Saihōji. Another temple of outstanding fame is Saihōji, or Kokedera – the Moss Temple. The upper garden has a Zen dry garden, the lower garden is completely covered by more than one hundred different species of green and yellow mosses.

Many temples charge a fairly modest admission fee. The entrance fee for Saihōji, however, is above average.

The Imperial Villas. To visit either the Katsura or Shugakuin Imperial villas you must apply for a pass to The Imperial Household Agency, Kyoto Gyoen Nai, Kamigyo-ku, Kyoto (tel. 075–211–1211). Apply two to five days before an intended visit. (Note that children are not admitted.) Both villas have exquisite gardens – the model of many in Japan.

The Byodoin Temple is situated in Uji City 15 kilometres south of Kyoto. You can reach Uji by rail (the Nara line). The temple is noted for its Ho-o-Do or Phoenix Hall, built in the eleventh century.

The Fushimi Inari Shrine is a short walk from Inari Station on the south side of Kyoto (Nara line from Kyoto Station). The striking feature of the Fushimi Inari Shrine is the approach through 10,000 red *torii* (see p.113) which stretch over 4 kilometres.

Trips from Kyoto

Nara. If you start early, you can cover a great deal of Nara in a one-day trip from Kyoto. You can either go to Nara from Kyoto by the JNR line (50 minutes) or by the more luxurious Kintetsu-Nara line (35 minutes).

The great delight of Nara is that it contains a huge deer park with over 1,000 tame deer. You can walk through the park to reach many of the places of interest. Near Kofukuji Temple is the Nara Tourist Office, which supplies enthusiastic guides to Nara (a free service).

The Kofukuji Temple is now only a shadow of what it once was (it originally had 175 buildings). Its five-storey pagoda, built in the fifteenth century, is very graceful, and its reflection in the nearby Sarusawa pond is one of the most popular sights in Japan.

Nara National Museum. Near Kofukuji Temple is the Nara National Museum, which is rich in art treasures from the Nara period (710–84). It is one of the finest museums in Japan, and open daily 9 am – 4.30 pm, except Mondays.

The Todaiji Temple has both the world's largest wooden structure and bronze statue of Buddha. The Buddha weighs 7.2 tonnes and is 15.5 metres high. The whole place is quite awesome for visitors today, but you wonder how it must have seemed to the people of Japan when it was first revealed in 752.

The Kasuga Shrine is one of the great Shinto shrines of Japan. Its main buildings date from the eighth century. Altogether the shrine has 3,000 stone and metal lanterns, which are lit at the shrine's great festivals (for example, the Mandoro Festival, on 3 February).

Horyuji. Some 45 minutes by bus from the Kintetsu Nara station is the Horyuji or Ikarugadera Temple. The temple has many sculptures and works of art of national importance, and is mentioned in Japan's oldest book, the *Nihonshoki*, or *Chronicles of Japan*, written in 720. In this area there are a number of other important temples, including the Chuguji Temple, which can all be reached on foot.

Himeji is a stop on the Shinkansen line, and you could treat this as a day-trip from Kyoto or as a stop

on the journey to Hiroshima and the South. Himeji
has a superb castle, which many regard as the best in
Japan. The castle is known as the Shirasagijo or White
Egret, because from a distance it resembles the egret,
a bird common in the local rice fields. The castle is
huge and original in design, the five-storey keep being
built in 1609.

Osaka is the third city of Japan with over 2,600,000   *Osaka*
inhabitants. It has always been important in Japanese
history, and is thought of as 'the city of merchants'.
In the latter part of the sixteenth century Osaka was
the headquarters of Hideyoshi Toyotomi, who built
Osaka Castle, which is to this day the city's principal
landmark. The keep has been rebuilt as a faithful copy
of the 1586 original, and a large part of the massive
stone walls are of the original sixteenth-century
construction.

Osaka has a circular JNR railway line, which
makes it very easy to get around. Adjoining the
station is an area called Umeda, which has many
department stores and the city's business centre.
Perhaps the most important attraction is the Expo
Memorial Park, a legacy of the 1970 Exposition held
there. The Park combines a garden, a recreation
centre and several museums. From Osaka Port you
can take a boat to Shikoku and Kyushu.

Kobe can be reached easily by train from Osaka or   *Kobe*
Kyoto. It is built on several hills and has a superb
harbour. It is somewhat like Yokohama, in that it is a
port which became a centre for the foreign merchants
who came to Japan to trade in the last century.

Kobe is a pleasant city with a cosmopolitan
atmosphere and is a place that foreigners always find
easy to live in. The cuisine offers some of the best
food in Japan. Kobe beef is particularly famous (and
expensive). From Kobe you can take a cruise on the
Inland Sea and boats to Shikoku and Kyushu.

Travelling from Tokyo you pass through the large   **Chubu**
region of Chubu. Chubu means 'middle' (as does the
name of another of Japan's regions, Chugoku), and is
divided into three sub-districts – the Tokai, the

Central Mountain and the Hokuriku districts. Each has its own distinctive character. Tokai has a beautiful coastline (especially in Shizuoka prefecture). The Central Mountain District (the Japan Alps or Chubu-Sangaku) has some of the highest mountains in Japan, and the area is one of the country's most popular tourist centres. Hokuriku is the region of Chubu along the Japan Sea Coast. This area has a lot of snow in winter (as much as 200 centimetres in some places).

Ise and Toba   Ise is 1 hour and 30 minutes by train from Nagoya, and if you want, you can change from the Tokyo to Ise train without leaving Nagoya Station. Ise has a number of impressive Shinto shrines set in beautiful woodland.

You can reach Toba from Ise either by train or by taking a scenic bus ride (30 minutes). Toba is the home of the pearl, and you can see all stages of the industry in progress, from the irritation of the oyster to the exchange of pearls for travellers' cheques. There are some lovely hotels in Toba, but the budget-conscious should stay in Ise!

Takayama   Takayama is a beautiful old town, which can be reached via Gifu in 3 hours by train from Nagoya. The area around the town is famous for its houses with steep-sided roofs (the *gassho-zukuri* style). The houses are enormous and a reminder of the days when the extended Japanese family lived together.

Kanazawa   You can travel to Kanazawa from Takayama via Toyama, and extend the trip by going on to Kyoto via Fukui, instead of returning to Nagoya. (Kanazawa is 6 hours and 30 minutes direct by train from Tokyo.) Kanazawa has many old buildings and the feel of another age.

Kamikochi   A favourite destination for those exploring the Japan Alps is the beautiful town of Kamikochi. Mountaineers often head to Kamikochi to begin their climb.

Karuizawa   Karuizawa is 2 hours 10 minutes from Tokyo, and is a popular holiday resort, especially in the summer and

with young people. It has always been a fashionable
spot, and many wealthy foreign visitors stayed there
in the last century. More recently the Crown Prince
of Japan met his future wife (the present Crown
Princess) on the tennis courts of the town, which lies
at the foot of the densely forested Mount Asama.

Chugoku is the region west of Kansai. A major **Chugoku**
industrial belt stretches from Kobe to Okayama and
Hiroshima. Chugoku contains many historical and
picturesque sites. The whole of the Inland Sea area
constitutes a protected natural park. The weather is
warm and the Japanese are justified in looking upon
the Inland Sea as their Mediterranean. The name for
the district lying principally on the south side of
Chugoku along the Inland Sea is San-Yo or the area in
the sun. By contrast the northern coastal area of
Chugoku and part of Kinki along the Japan Sea are
known as San-In or the area in the shadow of the
mountain.

You can take the train to the delightful town of *Kurashiki*
Kurashiki by changing from the Shinkansen at
Okayama station. In Kurashiki you should see the
Ohara Art Gallery built by a Japanese (and not an
Irish!) magnate in 1930, Mr Magosaburo Ohara. The
museum is in the form of a Greek temple, and houses
a huge collection of western art. Also of note is the
Kurashiki Folkcraft Museum. (Both museums are
closed on Monday.)

The Peace Memorial Park in Hiroshima covers the *Hiroshima*
area which was at the centre of the atomic blast. In the
park there are a number of monuments and the Peace
Memorial Museum. The city is lively and pleasant,
and if American visitors in particular are worried at
their reception in Hiroshima or Nagasaki, there is no
need for concern.

Miyajima is an island 20 kilometres south of *Miyajima*
Hiroshima. You can take a train from Hiroshima to
Miyajimaguchi and then the ferry to the island.

Miyajima is covered in woodland, and Mount Misen at its centre rises to 530 metres (1,740 feet).

The Itsukushima shrine on the island is one of the greatest shrines of Japan. Its torii stand in the sea at high tide and are 16 metres high. They are one of the *Nihon Sankei* or the three most celebrated sights in Japan. The shrine buildings are also built over the beach, so that at high tide the whole shrine seems to be floating on the sea. The shrine was founded in the sixth century and considerably enlarged in the twelfth.

San-In   The JNR line hugs the shore along the north coast of Chugoku, and a number of interesting places, which may seem remote, can be visited easily.

Matsue   Matsue is sometimes called 'the City of Water' or 'the Venice of Japan'. The city has many well-preserved buildings and a very fine seventeenth-century castle.

Among the famous residents of Matsue was Lafcadio Hearn (1850–1904), a Britisher, who came to Japan in the nineteenth century and wrote on many aspects of the country. He fell in love with Japan, married a Japanese woman and took out Japanese citizenship, adopting the name, Yakumo Koizumi. He has been an object of fascination in Japan (and outside it) ever since. The Yakumo Memorial House in Matsue displays a collection of his manuscripts which make fascinating reading. (They can easily be bought in paperback in Japan.) Hearn was enchanted with Japan until a profound disillusionment overcame him in his later life, when it seemed to him that the traditional life of the country which had so fascinated him was disappearing for ever.

Izumo   The Izumo Taisha Shrine is about an hour from Matsue and is the oldest Shinto shrine in Japan. Most of the shrine buildings were erected in 1874, though some are older than this. However, the *style* of the architecture is representative of the very earliest known in Japan.

Amano-hashidate   You can travel via Toyooka to Amanohashidate or go there from Kyoto. This is one of the Nihon Sankei. It is a slim sand bar in the sea, 3.6 kilometres long and covered in fantastically shaped pine trees. Visitors are recommended to look at the scene between their legs, and then Amanohashidate should appear suspended between sea and sky!

The island of Shikoku has four prefectures – Shikoku itself means four provinces. The island is famous among the Japanese as a place of pilgrimage, having 88 sacred temples. It is one of the four main islands of Japan and there are numerous ferry links with Honshu, the largest of the islands. Takamatsu is the principal city.   **Shikoku**

Kyushu is accessible by train, plane and boat. It is the southernmost of Japan's four islands, and has the warmest climate. It is rich in places of scenic and historical interest. The Shinkansen goes to Kitakyushu and Fukuoka, major industrial centres with coalmining areas nearby. Nagasaki is a major port.   **Kyushu**

Nagasaki is one of Japan's oldest and busiest ports, first opened to foreign trade in 1511. It is a lovely city with many places of interest. Sofukuji Temple was built in 1629, and is known as Nankindera or the Chinese Temple because of the Chinese influence on its architecture. Oura Catholic Church is built in the Gothic style, and is the oldest wooden (Christian) church in Japan. It was built to commemorate the deaths of 26 Christian martyrs crucified in 1597 after the outlawing of Christianity. The Glover Mansion near the Catholic church was the residence of a British merchant, Thomas Glover. It is said that the Glover mansion was the setting for Puccini's *Madame Butterfly*; it is indeed a fairy-tale location, and you could easily imagine Butterfly being there even if this were not the case.   *Nagasaki*

The Peace Park commemorates the site of the atomic explosion in August 1945.

This is an interesting town, 1 hour 48 minutes by train from Fukuoka. It has been called 'a city of woods and water' because of the abundant green groves. The most notable building in Kumamoto is   *Kumamoto* the castle, which has been rebuilt in the nineteenth and twentieth centuries.

Mount Aso You can go by bus from Kumamoto to Mount Aso, set in the Aso National Park. Aso is a volcano, and one of its peaks, Mount Nakadake, is still furiously active. Sightseeing is carefully organized.

Beppu Beppu is one of the best known spas in Japan. There are not only hot water baths but also hot sand baths. There are too a number of hells or Jigoku, which are boiling ponds, sometimes of coloured water and some spouting mud into the air.

Tohoku Tohoku means east and north, and Tohoku is the region occupying the northern part of Honshu. It is beautiful, unspoilt and relatively sparsely populated. The major cities are Sendai and Aomori. The Sendai area is extremely industrial, but nearby is Matsushima, one of the Nihon Sankei. This beautiful place is a bay scattered with small islands covered in pine trees. Not far from Sendai is Hiraizumi, an old town once owned by the Fujiwara family, who in the twelfth century founded the great Chusonji Temple. But the real charm of Tohuku lies in the small villages and huge areas of unspoilt country; perhaps the Japan many have come thousands of miles to see.

Hokkaido Hokkaido is the second largest island after Honshu. It means north land, and constitutes one huge prefecture. It was considered a frontier area until the last century and offers unique sights in Japan – large fields and herds of cows. Hokkaido has important lumber and fish canning industries and also coalmining. The major city is Sapporo, the fastest growing city in Japan recently overtaking Kyoto in the size of its population.

Hokkaido has a lot of snow in winter and is popular with skiers. In the summer it is cool and attracts people who want to escape from the heat of central and southern Japan.

Off the Hokkaido coast lie the Kurile Islands, taken from the Japanese by the Russians in 1945, and which the Japanese strongly believe should be returned to them.

Nearer to Taiwan than the Japanese mainland are the Okinawa Islands (part of the Nansei Islands). The Okinawa Islands constitute a tropical paradise for holiday-makers. Okinawa was an independent kingdom from the fourteenth to the nineteenth centuries (though throughout it had to pay tribute to Japan and sometimes to China). To this day, Okinawa has retained its own culture and Okinawans still have a language of their own.

Okinawa

Okinawa was the scene of some of the most horrific episodes of the Second World War, when in 1945 many thousands of Japanese to avoid surrender to the Americans committed suicide. This has left a legacy of sadness amidst the great beauty of the island. America occupied the island until 1972 when it reverted to Japan. Today one of the United States' largest military bases in the Far East is on Okinawa.

Historical highlights

Japanese history is divided into a number of distinct periods, largely deriving from the location of the seat of government.

Early history	to AD 710	
Nara	710–794	
Heian	794–1192	
Kamakura	1192–1336	Throughout this period
Muromachi	1336–1573	the 'bakufu' (military
Azuchi-Momoyama	1573–1603	government) and the
Edo or Tokugawa	1603–1868	imperial court were
Meiji	1868–1912	separate, the latter
		remaining in Kyoto.

A period of history may be more closely defined by reference to the reign of a particular emperor. In this century the Japanese use terms with which we are familiar, as their history has become one with the world's, thus: pre-war, interwar, postwar, etc.

The names taken by the emperor on his accession are also used to define periods of this century:

Meiji	–1912
Taisho	1912–1926
Showa	1926–

The Japanese use both the western way of naming years (that is, from the birth of Christ) and their own system, which is based on counting the year from the accession of the monarch. Thus 1986 is also called Showa 61.

In this book, when talking of emperors and other prominent historical figures, the first name will precede the family name. The Japanese usually put the family name first, and they never have more than one first name. Most Japanese only got a family name in the last century. Thus to have had a family name at all was a mark of distinction.

In the Stone Age Japan was inhabited by a people
called the Ainu. They were gradually displaced by
settlers from China and Korea, who arrived in
Kyushu and Southern Honshu. There may also have
been settlement by people from the Southern Pacific.
The Ainu were driven northward to colder and
poorer lands, which the Japanese did not become
seriously interested in until modern times. The Ainu
still exist as a separate racial and linguistic group in
very small numbers in Hokkaido. By AD 700 at the
latest immigration to Japan had ceased, and no other
large groups came to Japan until this century.

**Early history
(to AD 710)**

According to mythology the first Japanese emperor
was the Emperor Jinmu, who as great-grandson of
the Sun Goddess founded the imperial dynasty in 660
BC. As a definite fact much of Japan had been unified
by the fourth century by rulers whose political base
was in the Yamato Plain near Nara. The Yamato
dynasty began the line of emperors which has reigned
in unbroken succession to the present day. (Explana-
tions for this phenomenon have varied from the
Japanese having an enduring reverence for the Imperial family to the view that because the emperor was
for most of history lacking in power, abolition or
usurpation of the throne was never necessary.)

The emperor

Outsiders often confuse things Japanese and Chinese.
Japan and China are distinct and separate civiliza-
tions. That said, however, the Japanese have often
looked to China as the great teacher, and one aspect
of the modern Japanese view of China is to accord
China the same sort of respect that North Europeans
give to Ancient Greece and Rome.
    Buddhism was officially introduced to Japan
through China and Korea in AD 552. The new
religion received massive encouragement from a
brillant member of the Japanese Imperial family,
Prince Shotoku (who died in 622). He issued a
Seventeen-article Constitution in 604 based on
Buddhism and Chinese political theory. Monks
introduced the Chinese system of writing with
characters, which was gradually adopted by the

*Chinese
influence*

Japanese. But though Chinese culture had a deep and permanent infuence on Japan, political ideas were less successful. However, there was an attempt to give Japan a highly centralized and bureaucratic structure like China's, and part of this scheme was the foundation of a national capital.

Nara
(710–794)
A permanent
capital

Before 710 it was the practice of the Japanese to shift the capital on the death of the emperor; according to teaching at that time, the ruler's death made the capital impure. With the aim of centralizing and strengthening the national government, it was decided in 710 to fix one place as the centre of religious and political life. Nara became the first capital of Japan, and remained so until 794, when the emperor and court left Nara seeking independence from what had become (and still is) a Buddhist stronghold.

The arts

The Nara period is rich in art and architecture. A rapid building programme gave Nara an extraordinary collection of temples. In 752 the largest bronze Buddha in the world was cast and housed in Todaiji, itself the world's largest wooden structure.

Heian
(794–1192)
Heian, Kyoto
and Ch'angan

The emperor moved the capital from Nara to nearby Heian-Kyo, which was later known as Kyoto. This city remained the capital of Japan (that is the official residence of the Emperor) until 1868. Clearly, Kyoto has a supremely important place in Japanese history.

Heian, which is a synonym for Tang Ch'angan, the Chinese capital, was laid out on a grand scale with a symmetrical street pattern after Tang Ch'angan's. The Heian period is synonymous with a flowering and extreme refinement of the arts, and it is interesting to reflect that while courtiers wrote diaries in the seclusion of their gardens in Heian, on the other side of the world the Vikings were pillaging England.

The Fujiwara

The power of the emperors, always limited, grew weaker at this time, and a noble family, the Fujiwara (the wealthiest landowners in the country), virtually took over the running of the country. They were an able and astute family and did much to advance the refinement of culture in the Heian period. They also hit on the ingenious idea of continually marrying their daughters into the Imperial family and giving early retirement to any emperor who did not suit their purposes.

The late Heian period was wracked by civil war. Two noble families, the Minamoto based in eastern Japan and the Taira in the west, were the principal contenders for power. By 1156 the Taira had defeated their enemies and swiftly took control of the court in Kyoto. Kiyomori Taira's supremacy was later challenged by Yoritomo Minamoto, who in a bitter struggle from 1180 to 1185 seized power and proceeded to eliminate the entire Taira clan. Yoritomo established control over all Japan and made Kamakura (and not Kyoto) his capital. Perhaps he chose Kamakura because it had a superb defensive position – fringed by a circle of mountains and with the sea on one side. The emperor and the Fujiwara remained respected but powerless figures in Kyoto, while the Minamoto took effective power and the title of Shogun (equivalent to supreme general). On the death of Yoritomo in 1199 power fell into the hands of his wife's family (who were descendants of the Taira!). The Hojo family exercised effective control over Japan for the next century and a half.

Kamakura (1192–1336) *The Minamoto*

Kamakura quickly became a graceful city. In the Kamakura period monks came from south China, in support of newly established Buddhist sects. The most important of these was Zen which, with its emphasis on austerity and self-discipline, held a lasting appeal for Japan's warrior class. The Zen monks introduced tea drinking and also the art of dry gardening with rocks and stones.

Zen, tea and gardening

In the Kamakura period Japan faced its greatest threat from outside, until present times. Kubla Khan, who had conquered China and Korea and who became first of the Mongol line of Emperors in China, launched great invasions against Japan in 1274 and

Kamikaze

1281. The first invasion force had to withdraw because of stormy weather, and the second (numbering 150,000 men) was devastated by a typhoon, which the Japanese called *Kamikaze* or the divine wind. A myth grew up that the country was under the sacred protection of the gods.

Go-Daigo and the rise of the Ashikaga

The Kamakura system was severely strained by the preparations it made to meet the Mongol threat of Kubla Khan's. The Emperor Go-Daigo, taking advantage of Kamakura's weakness, tried to revive imperial authority and raised an army which took control of western Japan. The Shogun sent a general, Takauji Ashikaga, to fight the emperor. But Takauji changed sides. However, he had no intention of re-establishing imperial control and took political power for himself. He suppressed the Kamakura regime, destroyed the Hojo family and established his shogunate in Kyoto in 1336, thus decisively bringing the Kamakura period to an end.

Muromachi (1336–1573)

The Ashikaga clan ruled from a place outside Kyoto called Muromachi. Against a background of war and civil disorder (parts of Kyoto itself were destroyed during fighting) the Muromachi period witnessed important developments in the arts. There was the formation of Noh drama and the tea ceremony, and important developments in flower arranging and gardening. The Ashikaga lived splendidly and built many of the places in Kyoto which are landmarks today, for example Kinkakuji and Ginkakuji – the Gold and Silver Pavilions. In contrast to the wealth of the shoguns, the emperor and Imperial court were poverty-stricken, and stories were later told (by outraged imperialists) of how the emperor was forced to sell examples of his calligraphy to eke out a living.

The authority of the Ashikaga was threatened increasingly by the power of the great nobility or daimyo. They built up large armies of professional soldiers or samurai. In 1542 (or 1543) the first Europeans landed in Japan. These were the Portuguese. Curiously, of all the things they brought with them the most significant were guns and the Bible.

The guns were bought by the daimyo and their power was thereby augmented. Civil war intensified.

The Azuchi-Momoyama period is often seen as an extension of the former period and the whole known as: the Muromachi and Azuchi-Momoyama periods.

Azuchi-Momoyama (1573–1603)

The late sixteenth century was of great importance in Japanese history, for three remarkable leaders arose in succession to unite the country. Unified, Japan was in a position to determine her own future, and she did not become an imperial possession of western powers as, under different circumstances, she might have done.

> Nobunaga planted the rice and reaped it,
> Hideyoshi made it into rice cakes,
> And Ieyasu ate them.
> (old Japanese saying)

The first maker of national unity was Nobunaga Oda, a lord from the Nagoya region, who systematically defeated the shogun's enemies, and who, in the process, made himself rather than the shogun ruler of Japan. In 1582 he was assassinated.

One of Nobunaga's generals, however, Hideyoshi Toyotomi, who had made the remarkable ascent from peasant soldier, completed Nobunaga's work and totally reunited Japan by miltary conquest. In 1592 he embarked on the invasion of Korea. The Japanese armies killed many Koreans, and Hideyoshi's invasion is still viewed as one of the unfortunate milestones in Korean-Japanese relations. In 1598 on Hideyoshi's death, the Japanese pulled out of Korea and did not embark on another foreign venture until the nineteenth century (1874, the conquest of Taiwan).

The third and most famous of the makers of a unified Japan, and of course of his own fortune, was Ieyasu Tokugawa. He capitalized on Hideyoshi's sudden death and defeated the forces loyal to Hideyoshi's family. In 1603 Ieyasu was appointed shogun by the emperor, and his family, the Tokugawa, kept Japan in their grip until they surrendered power in the nineteenth century.

Edo or Tokugawa Japan (1603–1868)
Edo

The Tokugawa established their capital in Edo, the Tokyo of today. They turned it from a village into a huge and thriving city. The aristocracy were obliged to stay part of the year in Tokyo, and when they returned to their estates, they had to leave their close family behind to guarantee their political orthodoxy while they were away. As a result Tokyo became a city of pleasure. The aristocracy lived gorgeously.

Life in Edo was marked by boisterous festivals, geishadom, and the kabuki theatre. Far away in Kyoto in great dignity but utterly powerless throughout the Edo period the emperors presided over their court.

Feudalism or Shi Nō Kō Shō

The Tokugawa established a complex and successful system of government. It was highly conservative, and while European countries were developing fast in science and industry, Japan ossified. The Japanese were divided into four classes: warrior, farmer, artisan and merchant (Shi Nō Kō Shō), with the warrior (or samurai or bushi) at the top. The samurai strictly adhered to an unwritten code called the *bushido* or way of the warrior, which ordained selfless loyalty to superiors and the perfection of a martial spirit and skills (see *The martial arts, Leisure, Pleasure and Sport*). They were readily identifiable by their distinctive dress and their exclusive right to carry swords. The government prohibited movement between classes, but this proved impossible to enforce as members of the merchant class (whose wealth grew rapidly in the Edo period) married into the samurai class (which conversely suffered economically because of its divorce from all commercial activity).

Under the same government, contact with the outside world was all but stopped. Of westerners, only the Dutch were allowed small but highly regulated trading privileges, and were allowed only one trading post on a small island in Nagasaki harbour. Foreigners living in Japan were expelled, while Japanese people living abroad had to stay there; if they returned to Japan they were executed. Christianity was entirely suppressed.

Enough information seeped into Japan in the *The end of* nineteenth century to show a small group how far *isolation* behind the West Japan was technologically and scientifically. However, because the control of the Tokugawa was so tight, it was impossible to end the isolation from inside Japan. The shogunate was only forced to change its policy when, in 1853, Commodore Perry arrived with a US fleet (Japanese called them the Black Ships) and demanded trade concessions and the use of a Japanese port. (The Americans were vastly superior militarily to the Japanese, who were equipped with very much the same kinds of guns and swords they had had in the seventeenth century.)

After agreeing to US demands the government found itself obliged to grant similar concessions to European powers. The authority of the shogunate crumbled, as it was attacked both by those who blamed it for letting the foreigners in and by those who saw it as an obstacle to modernization. Civil war followed.

A group of determined imperialists seized control of **The Meiji** the Imperial court, and in January 1868 announced **Restoration** Japan's return to direct imperial rule. They carried **1868** out what is now known as the Meiji Restoration after *The Emperor* the name of the emperor. At the time the Emperor *Meiji* Meiji was only in his mid-teens. He was installed in the Tokugawa's castle at Edo (the Imperial Palace of today); Edo became the capital of Japan and was renamed Tokyo or Eastern capital.

The shogunate was abolished. The daimyo surren- *Changes* dered their power to the new government. In 1871 Japan was divided into the prefectures that exist today ruled by officials appointed in Tokyo. Though the samurai lost their privileges, many of them found a new place in society as bureaucrats and businessmen. Japan adopted a western-style constitution, taking elements from the governmental systems of the US and western European nations. (The Prussian constitution proved the greatest influence – a solidly conservative model with a highly restricted franchise.)

The government directed the industrialization of the country, and the 'ministerial guidance' of Japanese business and industry today should be seen as part of this long-established method of doing things in Japan. There is no doubt that Japan's legacy from the Tokugawa period – an educated elite, a sense of order and skills in government – made an enormous contribution to Japan's phenomenal development. Japan became the only non-western country to catch up with the West.

Empire and war The story of Japan's modern development is perhaps a familiar one. In two spectacular wars Japan defeated China (1894–5) and Russia (1904–5). She began to acquire an empire in order to supply raw materials and markets. By the end of the First World War she had annexed Formosa, Korea and parts of China. Thereafter there were two important turning-points.

1931 In 1931 the military seized the initiative from democratic politicians in Japan and embarked energetically on foreign conquests. But Japan found itself in increasing difficulties in China, where the rise of nationalism meant the beginning of fierce resistance to the invading Japanese.

1941 The West and the US in particular was increasingly uneasy at Japan's policies, and by 1941 the US had cut off oil supplies to Japan. Japan's attack on the American fleet on 8 December 1941 (7th in the West) at Pearl Harbor was a vast gamble: the Japanese military relied on the Americans having neither the determination nor stamina to fight a long Pacific war. On 15 August 1945 (14th in the West) the emperor asked the Japanese people to accept the unacceptable and surrender. Japan had been devastated by war and was the first victim in the world of atomic destruction.

Modern Japan *The new constitution* In 1947 the Japanese adopted a new constitution, which despite the omnipresence of the Americans looked remarkably British. Everyone gained the right to vote including women, and the prefects became directly accountable to voters rather than being appointed by the central government. The emperor became a symbol of the nation, without political power (which in fact throughout history he had nearly always been). A prime minister and cabinet initiated policy and the National Diet was accorded similar powers to those of the Westminster Parliament (though the Japanese House of Councillors, the upper house, is elected and has more power than the British House of Lords).

An article in the constitution renounced war forever and forbade the build-up of war potential. However, Japan has since steadily increased its military forces (under US pressure), although military questions have been perhaps the most divisive in Japanese politics.

Land ownership was radically altered during the occupation. Great estates were broken up and the countryside became the society of small farmers that it is today. The Americans abolished the *zaibatsu* or huge industrial conglomerates, which they thought had fuelled the imperialism of pre-war Japan. Many zaibatsu regrouped even while the Americans were in Japan.

Economic reforms

The immediate postwar political scene was at times turbulent, with large-scale trade union action. In the 1960s there were vigorous protests among students and radicals at US foreign politics in Vietnam for example. But arguably the most important event of Japanese political life is that a conservative coalition, the Liberal Democratic Party (the LDP), was founded in 1955 and has held power continuously since then. (Indeed, during the postwar period right-wing political views have prevailed throughout Japan). Although the countryside is conservative and overrepresented in the Diet at the expense of the towns, Japanese society as a whole seems remarkably right-wing. Extreme political stability and the close co-operation of government and industry have been the principal foundation of Japan's postwar development.

Politics

Oil shocks and prosperity   The steep rise in oil prices in 1973–4 caused a deep economic crisis in Japan and exposed Japanese dependence on overseas oil. (Japan imports nearly all the raw materials used by industry.) Japan coped remarkably well by restructuring her industry to make it more efficient in the use of energy. Similarly, Japan weathered the oil shock of 1979 in the wake of the Iranian revolution. Today Japan finds her oil bills decreasing and her balance of payments showing (embarrassingly) huge surpluses.

A religious note

This section is designed to help with visits to shrines and temples, which will probably be an important part of your stay in Japan. The two major religions of the country are Shinto and Buddhism. For most Japanese adherence to Shinto and Buddhism is not thought incompatible, and so the two religions play a part in the lives of most Japanese. The place of worship of Shinto is the shrine, immediately recognizable by its distinctive gateway or *torii*, and the place of worship of Buddhism is the temple. The philosophy of Confucianism has also played an important role in the history and development of Japan. There are very few Christians in Japan, but Japanese people are aware of and generally respect the tenets of Christianity (but find its exclusivity difficult to accept).

Shinto or Shintoism

Shinto is indigenous to Japan and has not travelled outside the country (except for a short period before the last war). It is a religion without doctrines or creeds. It venerates the spirit of nature, which is thought to manifest itself in natural phenomena. Shrines are very often places of exceptional calm or beauty where nature is manifest. They are also the home of the spirit of an outstanding figure, a prince or warrior, for example. Shinto is an optimistic religion; it believes in continual renewal. Thus, for example, an earthquake is not the judgement of god, but part of life's cycle, and what is destroyed can be built again.

The emperor is the major figure in Shinto, and was until the end of the war a divine figure. The close identification of the Shinto religion and the state is, however, quite recent, occurring only with the rise of nationalism at the end of the Meiji era.

Shinto priests can marry, and the religion plays an

important part in the community. New-born babies are brought to the shrine, while Shinto weddings are the most common in Japan. The site of new buildings is usually blessed by a Shinto priest.

Buddhism Buddhism came to Japan in the sixth century. It offers a system of belief and teaching by which a person might gain enlightenment. Buddhism has been important in strengthening the sense of family and in developing ancestor worship.

The Buddhist monasteries had great political power until the Tokugawa period (1603–1868), when they were forced to surrender authority to the shogunate. The Meiji reformers largely looked upon Buddhism as an old-fashioned creed and a hindrance to development; many temples were destroyed.

Some Buddhist temples are reputedly very rich. Buddhism is almost totally in control of funeral ceremonies, and most Japanese wish to have family graves in a Buddhist cemetery. The Buddhist clergy are allowed to marry except for some higher clergy and monks.

Confucianism Confucius lived in China from approximately 551 to 479 BC. His writings taught that society was naturally ordered and hierarchical and that the people owed loyalty to the ruler, children to their father and pupils to their teacher. Confucianism was strongly favoured by the Tokugawa Shogunate. Today very few people subscribe to Confucianism, but its paternalistic attitudes are part of the fabric of Japan, manifest in respect for the law, loyalty to one's company and veneration for education.

Shrines (jinja) Shrines tend not to have old buildings. Shinto is a religion of renewal and, logically, buildings are renewed too. At the Grand Shrine of Ise all buildings are demolished and reconstructed in exactly the same form every twenty years. Visitors are welcomed to shrines and do not have to pay an entrance fee. Shrine and temple compounds are often lovely islands of peace amid the noise and frenzy of the cities.

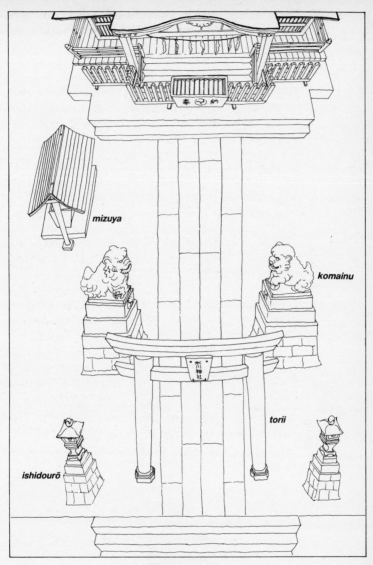

A Japanese shrine
© Hiroshi Umemura 1985

The entrance to shrines are the *torii* (gates), and *Torii* shrines on maps are marked by the symbol of torii. The torii divide the shrine, the purified place, from the unpurified place, the world.

Ishidourō   The characteristically Japanese stone lanterns, *ishi-dourō*, might be found at the entrance to the shrine or within the shrine compound.

Mizuya   Near the torii is the *mizuya* or water place, which is generally roofed over. Worshippers wash their hands there and purify their mouths before entering the shrine, and ladles are left at the mizuya for that purpose and not for drinking from.

Shimenawa   You may notice thick ropes or *shimenawa* tied between torii and between trees etc. in the shrine compound or sacred place. These are made of new rope every year and denote a purified place. Shide, white paper or cotton hangings, and branches of the *sakaki* tree, called *tamagushi*, are often attached to the shimenawa. It was thought that the gods descended into the sakaki tree.

Komainu   The two animals in the form of lions/dogs standing guard at the entrance to the main buildings of the shrine.

A komainu
© Hiroshi Umemura 1985

The main building of the shrine. Inside you see *Honden* offerings of fruit, flowers, sake, etc. and in the centre there is usually a mirror to symbolize the presence of the god or gods in the shrine. You do not enter the *honden*, but offer prayers by the *saisen bako*.

This is the offertory box. It is customary to throw in a *Saisen bako* few coins, clap hands three times, bow one's head and say a silent prayer. The jingling of the coins in the box is supposed to attract the god's attention. You may also shake the bell rope by the saisen bako if you think that alone will not work.

These are small wooden tablets seen hanging up in *Ema* rows on boards around the shrine compound. *Ema* means picture of a horse, and the horse has a long association with shrines, at one time being used as a sacrifice to the shrine gods. People write their request to the gods on ema. These range from requests for good wives and husbands, to success in exams.

These are the papers on which predictions are *Omikuji* written. If a shrine has *omikuji*, you can pull a stick out of a box to receive your fortune paper. If the prediction is good you take the paper with you, but if it is bad you tie it to a tree in the shrine compound, thereby leaving the bad fortune behind.

By contrast with shrines, temples are ornate, and **Temples** often use the colours red, green and gold in deco- **(*o tera*)** ration. However, many temples have become rather subdued in colouring, and compared with those in other Buddhist countries Japanese temples may seem quiet, even sombre. Many Japanese temples are set in gardens which are world-famous, and no satisfactory history of gardening is complete without a chapter on the temple gardens of Kyoto.

On visiting a temple you may make a money offering as at a shrine, but you do not (usually) go through the ritual cleansing or clap your hands before praying. Often Japanese men and women light an incense stick before a Buddhist deity, and many also like to rub their hands in the incense smoke coming from the large incense burners on the main approach to the big temple.

Temples, which are often great repositories of art treasures, generally charge an entrance fee to visitors. When you go into the main temple buildings you must take off your shoes (and sometimes carry them around in a cellophane bag). Temple viewing in winter should only be undertaken in thick socks!

Sanmon The entrance to a temple is through a great gate called a *sanmon*, which means a gate in the mountains, as the first temples in Japan were built in the mountains and forests. The gatehouse is huge and is usually set in an impressive wall surrounding the temple compound.

Shoro In the temple grounds one will probably see a bell tower or *shoro* with a huge bell, which can be struck from the side. Striking this bell or *bonsho* is associated with striking against evil or helping in the salvation of a dead person. Generally, it is permissible for any visitor to strike the bell. (At New Year this is the bell which the priest or monk strikes 108 times.) The shoro also announced the time of day in the years before everyone possessed clocks and watches (like the church clock in the West).

Pagoda Within the grounds one might also see a pagoda, which was originally the place where relics were kept.

Hondo A large temple will probably have many buildings. The main one is called the hondo and is where the principal Buddhist image or *honzon* is kept. It is in front of this image that the priests hold services. Buddhist rituals involve much chanting and often music on instruments particular to Japanese Buddhism. A gong is struck to summon people to prayer.

Holidays and festivals

Businesses, banks, etc. are closed on:

1 January	New Year's Day
15 January	Coming-of-Age Day
11 February	National Foundation Day
21 March*	Vernal Equinox Day
29 April	Emperor's Birthday
3 May	Constitution Day
5 May	Children's Day
15 September	Respect-for-the-Aged Day
23 September*	Autumnal Equinox Day
10 October	Health and Sports Day
3 November	Culture Day
23 November	Labour Thanksgiving Day

* date varies from year to year.

**National
festivals**
*O Shogatsu –
New Year*

This officially lasts from 1–3 January, but goes on much longer. The Japanese people decorate the outsides of their houses and inside there is much eating of special food and sake drinking. It is customary for the Japanese to visit a shrine or temple and to pay their respects to relatives, boss, associates, etc. A company president may well spend ten days greeting the people connected with him.

At the stroke of midnight on New Year's Eve temple bells begin to strike 108 times to signify the elimination of the 108 desires of man. Most people stay up all night and quite a few go to a place, like the beach, where they can watch the new sun rising.

The visitor to Japan might feel a bit out of things at this time, as it is a great family occasion. However, the weather is brilliantly sunny (in Kanto and Kansai, for example) and there is a rich scene to observe.

Seijin-no-Hi – 15 January
Coming-of- This celebrates the day when boys and girls reach the
Age Day age of majority in Japan – their twentieth birthday.
Setsubun – *Setsubun* marks, somewhat optimistically, the last
bean throwing day of winter. The bean throwing is carried out with
vigour at homes, shrines and temples, and symbolizes
the driving out of evil spirits. Participants shout:
'Huku wa uchi oni wa soto' (welcome good fortune,
devil go away!).

Hina Matsuri 3 March
– Dolls' Festival This is the festival which falls on the third day of the
or Girls' Day third month. Old dolls are put on display in homes
and in such places as hotel lobbies.

Hanami – February-April
blossom Blossoms come out in succession in Japan: usually,
viewing plum (in February), followed by peach (March), and
cherry (late March – early April). They tend not to
last very long, the cherry particularly, which swamps
a place in white blossom for just a few days. The
Japanese, sensibly, take the opportunity to combine
blossom-viewing and a picnic. In Tokyo, the best
place to see cherry blossom is Ueno Park at the end of
March or the very beginning of April (but it is very
crowded).

O Higan March and September
O Bon 13–16 July and August
These two occasions are similar. *O Higan* is the time
when people visit the family graves to pay their
respects. At *O Bon* the spirits of ancestors are
believed to return to the earth. People go to their
home towns at this time to remember those who have
died in their family, often lighting a small fire outside
or a lantern inside to guide the spirits home.

Tango-no-sekku 5 May
– Boys' Festival Families with boys fly carp streamers, *koinobori*,
or Children's Day from their houses and treat boys to special foods and
sometimes a present.

29 April–5 May

Golden week is so called because three festivals occur in one week: the Emperor's Birthday (29 April), Constitution Day (3 May) and Boys' Festival (Children's Day) (5 May). The weather is glorious, and you should perhaps only contemplate travelling if you have seats reserved.

The emperor greets well-wishers on his birthday and at New Year from a window of the Imperial Palace in Tokyo. Visitors can join in with the crowds and pick up a flag to wave.

7 July, 6–8 August

The two stars Vega and Altair meet in the Milky Way on this day. (In Chinese mythology, a prince and his lover could only meet once a year like these stars.) Children write poems, copy out quotations and hang up their scripts on decorated bamboo branches. The Sendai festival is one of the great festivals of Japan.

15 November

This festival is held in honour of girls who are three and seven years old and boys who are five. The children dressed in kimonos or in their slightly Edwardian Sunday-best go with proud parents and grandparents to shrines to ask for good fortune. If you are a photographer, station yourself at the Meiji Shrine at this time.

25 December

Although most people go to work on Christmas Day, the Japanese enjoy many of the trappings of Christmas. Christmas becomes a kind of warm-up for O Shogatsu, the time of celebration in Japan.

A demand for chicken and ice-cream cake has been stimulated by manufacturers (with ice-cream makers keen to boost their sales at a slack time of year).

Local festivals

The list that follows can only hope to give a small selection of the local festivals that take place in Japan. Many of the greatest are held in the old cities of Kyoto and Nara, but every locality has its festival or *matsuri* where you may well encounter *mikoshi* or

portable shrines, being carried around the neighbourhood by enthusiastic (and increasingly inebriated)
bearers.

Dezomeshiki – Firemen's Parade, Tokyo (6 January)	Firemen perform remarkable acrobatic stunts at the top of bamboo ladders.
Festival of Mount Wakakusayama, Nara (15 January)	This festival is celebrated by setting the slopes of the hill on fire and with fireworks.
Snow Festival, Sapporo (2–6 January)	The biggest snow festival in Japan (perhaps in the world).
Mandoro – Lantern Festival, Kasuga Shrine, Nara (3 February)	Celebrated by the lighting of 3,000 ancient lanterns.
Takayama Matsuri (14–15 April)	A long procession of floats through this ancient town in Gifu Prefecture.
Cormorant fishing, Nagara River, Gifu Prefecture (11 May – 15 October)	Fishermen use blazing torches to attract the fish, which are caught by cormorants, but which they are not permitted to keep. (This style of fishing may now net more tourists than fish.)
Kanda Matsuri, Tokyo (15 May)	The first of Tokyo's three major festivals. The mikoshi of the Kanda Myojin Shrine are carried through Kanda.
Sanja Matsuri, Tokyo (17 and 18 May)	Following hot on the footsteps of the Kanda Matsuri this is another of Tokyo's big three. The Sanja Festival is held at the great Asakusa Shrine.

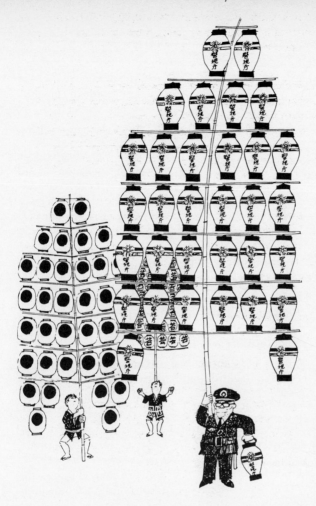

© John Weatherhill Inc.

Aoi Matsuri –
Hollyhock Festival,
Kyoto (15 May)

This is one of the most
ancient festivals in Japan,
dating back to the sixth

century when prayers were offered to the gods to plead for the ending of a time of great famine and drought. Abundant rains fell, and in their gratitude the Japanese people are said to have offered *aoi* or hollyhock leaves to the gods. Today the hollyhock is still used as the decorative motif of the festival. The main attraction is a replica of the ancient imperial carriage pulled by oxen.

Grand Festival of the Toshogu Shrine, Nikko (17–18 May)	A procession of samurai warriors in armour.
Sanno Festival, Akasaka, Tokyo (15 June in the lunar calendar)	The third of Tokyo's great festivals. Takes place at the Hie Shrine.
Kengensai – Music Festival, Itsukushima Shrine, Miyajima (mid-July)	An image of the shrine's deity travels by boat to the shrines on nearby islands.
Gion Matsuri, Kyoto (16–17 July)	Perhaps the greatest festival in Japan. Dates back to the Heian Period (794–1192) and was devised to seek the favour of the gods during the plague.
Nebuta Matsuri, Aomori (1–7 August)	Papier maché dummies or *nebuta* form a procession. The nebuta are usually figures of warriors to frighten away evil and protect the city.
Daimonji Bonfire, Kyoto (16 August)	Part of the O Bon Festival – the Chinese letter *Dai* (meaning large, great) is lit

up on the slopes of Mount Nyoigatake to bid farewell to souls after O Bon. The letter is formed from a series of bonfires, lit at night and visible from all parts of Kyoto.

Yabusame – horseback archery, Hachimangu Shrine, Kamakura (16 September)

An elaborate display of archery on horseback. The archers wear medieval costume and shoot with astounding accuracy.

Jidai Matsuri – The Festival of the Ages, Kyoto (22 October)

Procession in ancient costume from the Gosho to Heian Jingu in Kyoto.

Language, courtesies and pleasantries

The written language
Kanji

The Japanese imported and gradually adopted the Chinese writing system between the fifth and ninth centuries AD. The Chinese used characters or pictograms to write down their language, and many of the characters used in writing Chinese, Korean and Japanese are still the same. The Japanese call the Chinese characters used in their language *kanji*. There are thousands of kanji, but the basic number required to be able to read and write Japanese is about 2,000. A Japanese child has to know these to be able to graduate from school. (For examples of kanji, see *Japanese script: useful words and signs*.)

"Perhaps the medium is the message!"

Reproduced by courtesy of *Punch*

Kana In addition to kanji, the Japanese employ *kana* in writing. These are 'letters' rather than pictograms. There are two sets of kana, which are rather like our alphabet. The two syllabaries are known as *hiragana* and *katakana*. The forty-six kana in each syllabary can be learnt in a matter of weeks. Hiragana is used to write verb inflections, pronouns and particles. Katakana is used (today) to write down foreign words.

Although kana are commonly used in conjunction with kanji, the Japanese language could be written entirely in kana. This written language was devised in the ninth century, and some of the great writing of the Heian period was inscribed exclusively in kana script. (An important example is Lady Murasaki's 'The Tales of Genji' – the world's first novel.) You might wonder why the Japanese have not abandoned the complicated kanji for the straightforward kana, and indeed, have not opted for either hiragana or katakana. There is no doubt that, for the Japanese, kanji conveys a depth, feeling and clarity which the kana alone cannot express.

Learning kanji in itself has done much to shape the Japanese people. It has made them very visually minded; so that they often ask to see something written down and are extremely sensitive to form. The colossal task of memorizing kanji has also, perhaps, made them adept at other memory work, and it certainly calls for patience.

Romaji

The Japanese language is nowadays sometimes written in roman characters (i.e. our alphabet) rather than Japanese script. The Japanese call this *romaji*. For example, shop signs and the names of stations are often written this way, as are the Japanese words and phrases given in this book. (Nevertheless, the majority of Japanese still have some difficulty reading romaji.)

A guide to the pronunciation of romaji

1   As a rule each syllable is pronounced:

   I/gi/ri/su (England)   *A/me/ri/ka* (America)

2   The vowels (Japanese order given) are pronounced as follows:

   a   as in   bar
   i   as in   meet

u   as in   put
e   as in   met
o   as in   dot

3   The 'u' is often lost in pronunciation. *Desū* (is/are) is pronounced 'des'.

4   The distinction between long and short vowels is important:

obasan   (aunt, middle-aged woman)
obāsan   (grandmother, elderly woman)

5   The initial 'g' of a word is hard as in 'get'. Try saying, *ginko* (bank).

6   In Japanese 'r' is pronounced with the tip of the tongue hitting the ridge just behind the upper teeth. Foreign visitors find it almost impossible to get this right. Try saying *ringo* (apple/s).

7   The 'n' is nasal, as in the English word 'not'. Say, Nagasaki (the city of Kyushu).

8   The letter 'f' does not exist in Japanese, though it does appear in roman letters where it is pronounced rather lightly. Try saying *fūto* (envelope/s). The sound corresponding to 'f' is often written as an h. Thus, one encounters a word which can be written in two ways: for example, *hāfu* or *hāhu* (half).

9   Double consonants must be carefully pronounced, for example, *kis/saten* (coffee shop/s).

10   The question of intonation is complex. Generally, however, it is rather more flat than in English.

Some points of grammar

1   Verbs keep the same form in all persons. For example, *ikimasu* can mean I, he, she, it, you, they go or will go.

2   Personal pronouns are not used nearly as much in Japanese as in English. For example, in the sentence (*watashi wa*) *whisky o nomimasu* (I drink whisky), the words for I (*watashi wa*) can easily be omitted.

3   Singular and plural forms of nouns are often the same in Japanese. Thus, the word *mikan* means

orange and oranges, and *mikan o kudasai* means
an orange/some oranges please.
4   Verbs are usually placed at the end of a sentence.

Counting in Japan is a problem, as there are different   **Numbers and**
counting systems for different things, for example: **counting**

issatsu	1 book
hitori	1 person
ichinen	1 year
ippun	1 minute
ichizen	1 pair of chopsticks
ichiban	first

However, the commonest counters are used with
money, and this list forms the basis of all counting:

1	ichi	11	juuichi
2	ni	12	juuni
3	san	13	juusan
4	shi or yon	14	juushi or juuyon
5	go	15	juugo
6	roku	16	juuroku
7	shichi or nana	17	juushichi or
8	hachi		juunana
9	kukyu	18	juuhachi
10	juu	19	juuku

20	nijuu	100	hyaku
30	sanjuu	200	nihyaku
40	yonjuu	300	sanbyaku
50	gojuu	400	yonhyaku
60	rokujuu	500	gohyaku
70	shichijuu or	600	roppyaku
	nanajuu	700	nanahyaku
80	hachijuu	800	happyaku
90	kyujuu	900	kyuhyaku

1,000	sen	7,000	nanasen
2,000	nisen	8,000	hassen
3,000	sanzen	9,000	kyusen
4,000	yonsen	10,000	man or ichiman
5,000	gosen	20,000	niman
6,000	rokusen	1,000,000	hyaku man

Note that in Japanese there is a unit for 10,000. Larger numbers take account of this unit – for example, 1 million is 100 × 10,000.

Lucky and unlucky numbers

The number 1 is lucky, as it means 'best' or 'top'; 8 is also a good number, as the character which represents 8 means 'growth' and 'development'.

One of the words for 4, *shi*, also means 'death'. The number 9 is also unlucky since one meaning of the word for 9 is 'pain'. (49 is considered a particularly unlucky number.)

Imported language

The Japanese language has absorbed many words from other languages and most recently and most predominantly from English. Some of these words and expressions have been adopted with only a slight change in pronunciation and no change in meaning:

erebētā	elevator, lift
appuru pai	apple pie
sētā	sweater
basu	bus
depāto	department store

However, many words and phrases have undergone not only a change in pronunciation but also a change in meaning. Additionally, Japanese people have made up entirely new English-sounding words. These words are known collectively as *Japlish*. Here are some examples of the Japlish tongue:

jan pā	jacket (from jumper)
ji-pan	jeans
kahusu botan	cuff links
jūsu	any soft drink
high bowl	whisky and soda
hotto	hot coffee
tabako	cigarettes
gasorin sutando	garage
huronto garasu	windshield
beddo taun	dormitory town
manshon	western-style apartment
sarari man	office worker or employee

arubaito	part-time job (from the German, *arbeit*, meaning 'work')
bēsu appu	base up (pay increase)
feminisuto	a man who is kind to women
ōrudo misu	a spinster
sukin shippu	body contact
naitā	night game (of baseball)

The Japanese language is marked by a huge number of gradations in tone from the archly polite to the cosily familiar. A Japanese speaker must choose the right form depending on their relationship to the person addressed.

Striking the right tone

In general, a Japanese person will make what is theirs seem more humble and what belongs to another rather better. If this idea influences your English while you are in the country, it will help you appear more attuned to Japanese culture. In this way, the sentence 'This is really nothing' might disguise the fact that 'This is an expensive present'; and 'You know England so well' politely upgrade the fact that 'You know where England is'.

Modesty

In Japan the concept of 'self-modesty' is not only expressed as a matter of style, but often also by using separate vocabularies for what is yours (lower) and another person's (higher). Here are some examples:

Yours	Mine	
goshujin	*shujin*	(husband)
okusama	*kanai*	(wife)
otōsan	*chichi*	(father)
okāsan	*haha*	(mother)
otaku	*uchi*	(home/house or company/office)

The 'o' and 'go' in a word is often (and in all of the cases above) an honorific form.

Adult Japanese men and women rarely call each other by their first names. They use the family name with the suffix *san* (or *kun* or *chan* for younger members) or with the suffix *sensei* for teachers, doctors and other professionals. The use of titles is in keeping

Titles

with the importance they attach to modesty. You should never, for example, introduce yourself as Smith san but as Smith; on the other hand, you must be careful to call the other person Nakasone san and not Nakasone.

The Japanese have instinctively taken to using Mr, Mrs and Miss, perhaps because they feel they must automatically replace san with some other title.

His and hers The Japanese do not only have to choose between 'higher' and 'lower' vocabulary, there is also a distinct masculine and feminine vocabulary. For those people serious about learning Japanese, it is imperative to learn the right form. A woman using male vocabulary is considered coarse and uncivil. The man who uses women's vocabulary is said to have learnt his Japanese in bed.

Take the word 'I': we have seen that it has the form, *watashi wa*. Here are *some* of its other forms:

watakushi	(the same as *watashi*, formal male and female use)
jibun	(formal male use)
boku	(for informal friendly male use)
ore	(used by men speaking to close friends)
washi	(working class male use)
atai or atashi	(used by girls or women – slang)
uchi	(used by girls in Kansai only)

Disagreeing and agreeing The Japanese find it difficult to say no directly, and would rather avoid a quarrel. Instead of saying no (*iie*) a Japanese might say *chigaimasu* (it is different), look doubtful or remain silent.

Iie is much more likely to be heard twice in rapid succession in reply to fulsome thanks, as in the following exchange:

Sumimasen, dōmo, arigato gozaimasu (Really, thank you very much indeed).
Iie, iie (not at all).

The word yes (*hai*) is frequently used by the listener   *Saying yes*
to show that they are following in interested fashion
what is being said. It means: 'I understand what is
being said' rather than, 'I agree with what is being
said' (as many foreigners think).

Replies to negative questions are also apt to cause
confusion. Let us take a typical conversation on a
cold day:

It isn't very warm today.
Yes (Yes, you're right, it isn't very warm today).

A tricky habit for the Japanese to master (in   **Eye contact**
public-speaking competitions in Japan marks are
awarded for good eye contact). The Japanese often sit
and listen with their eyes down.

A smile can mean many things in Japan – embarrass-   **Smiling**
ment, shame, apology, uncertainty, nervousness. In
other words, a smile is used as a cover for uneasiness,
as well as, of course, as an expression of happiness.

Japanese people nod continuously to show they are   **Nodding**
listening attentively.

Japanese children are taught to sit up straight and to   **Posture**
look ahead of them. Men think it is good manners to
do the same and sit with their legs apart, not crossed.
(To the westerners this looks rather military.) Certainly it is not a good idea for foreign visitors to
slump in their seats at meetings or meals.

A delicate matter and one on which westerners can   **Bowing**
come unstuck. Visitors in particular should be discreet in bowing: bow slightly when using pleasantries, but do not bow too deeply or too often.

There are a large number of books that tell the   **Polite small**
Japanese how to entertain foreigners – about which   **talk**
they are often exceedingly nervous. You may be sure
that your visit will not be treated casually.

Conversations with new acquaintances generally
follow the same pattern:

1 Trouble will be taken to ensure that your first name and surname have been correctly heard and identified. (Remember that even Japanese names often cause confusion among other Japanese.)

2 You will be asked where you come from. Keep your answer simple: for the sake of clarity, name the nearest large city.

3 You will be asked whether you live alone or with your family. Any circumstances apart from these will provoke consternation – but perhaps this will change as Japan's horizons broaden year by year.

4 Questions about hobbies and interests are very important, as the answers indicate what sort of person you are. Therefore they must not be taken lightly. Japanese language programmes have drilled the following formula into their audiences: 'Excuse me, but may I ask what is your hobby?' (hobby meaning interests in general). An ideal answer might be: 'I like music, especially Beethoven, and I play golf whenever I have the opportunity. What is your hobby, if I may ask?'

5 You may be asked all kinds of general questions about your country. If your Japanese acquaintance lights on some unfortunate topic, it will only be because he or she is trying to find something pleasant to say: any offence will be quite unintentional.

6 You may be asked how old you are. Even if you are not questioned directly, your age will be a subject of interest and speculation, as age counts for a great deal in Japan, and status and treatment often depend on it. If (as is frequently the case with westerners) you turn out to be younger than your Japanese acquaintance has imagined, you may find that the atmosphere suddenly becomes more relaxed.

7 Westerners are sometimes taken aback by the frankness of some of the questions asked. Don't feel under any obligation to talk about subjects that make you feel uncomfortable. Most Japanese are very sensitive to reactions in others, and admire and cultivate the capacity to respond to other people's thoughts and feelings without resorting to words. Hence you may notice abrupt

changes of subject: the speed with which a Japanese person alters the course of a conversation indicates the degree of politeness involved.

People rarely drop in on each other unannounced in Japan; if they do visit each other in their homes, more protocol is observed by host and guest than in the West.

Visiting a Japanese home

The TIC runs a home-visit scheme (you must apply to join the scheme 24 hours in advance). Apart from this, the first-time visitor is unlikely to be offered a chance to visit the Japanese at home for a number of reasons. First, accommodation is a topic about which the Japanese are very sensitive in the company of westerners. The luxury of homes in the West has almost certainly been exaggerated in the minds of the Japanese, partly because of the image projected by commercials and partly because every Japanese knows the comment once made of Japan by EEC officials: that the country is peopled with workaholics who live in rabbit hutches. Second, an invitation to a Japanese home would probably necessitate quite a long journey – from central Tokyo, say, to the suburbs. Japanese thoughtfulness for a guest would tend to make a host hesitant to suggest this. Third, a Japanese hostess would be anxious that she could not offer her guest the range (and possibly the standard) of food available in a restaurant. Remember that a Japanese meal depends on a variety of dishes. Fourth and furthermore, many women would feel shy in the company of westerners. In their own homes they may be accustomed to serving food on their knees and in silence to honoured guests. Moreover, their lack of English would be thought an insuperable obstacle to the successful entertainment of a foreign guest.

Nevertheless, you may be lucky enough to receive an invitation to a Japanese home. When you go be sure to take a small gift with you – flowers, cakes, something for the house or for the children or a souvenir from your own country. You will be treated with the utmost civility and consideration, and the hospitality will be superb. In deference to the sensibilities of your host and hostess, resist the temptation to be casual in the western style. In particular you should bear in mind that Japanese women do not like people to intrude into their kitchens. There is a proverb that runs: *Gakuya-ura o nozoku* – 'It is bad manners to look backstage'.

Greetings and pleasantries

For polite phrases to be used before and after a meal, see p.45. You may also find the following phrases useful:

konnichi wa	hello (used all day until sunset)
ohayō or *ohayō gozaimasu*	good morning is pronounced in the same way as Ohio, the American state
konban wa	good evening
sayōnara	goodbye
o yasumi nasai	goodnight (said just before retiring to bed)
dōzo yoroshiku onegai shimatsu	I am very pleased to meet you (most polite)
yoroshiku	pleased to meet you (less polite)
dōmo	thank you
dōmo arigato	thank you very much
arigato gozaimasu	thank you very much indeed
dō itashimashite	you are welcome (said in reply to expression of thanks)
sumimasen	excuse me
dōmo sumimasen	excuse me (more emphatic, used to attract someone's attention or when you want to pass in front of someone)
gomen nasai	I am sorry, pardon me (for example, after treading on someone's foot)
dōzo (often used in combination)	please (a very popular word, used with other words) when offering something, when allowing someone to pass through a door, and so on)

dōzo osuwari kudasai	please sit down
dōzo meshiagatte kudasai	please start to eat
ogenki desuka?	how are you?
o kage sama de genki desu	I am very well (most polite)
genki desu	I'm fine (less polite)
o-jama shimasu	I am intruding (when entering a room as a guest)
yoku/yokoso irasshaimashita	I am pleased to see you
o-jama shimashita	I am leaving – really I have disturbed you (said by a departing guest)
mata dōzo	please come again
daijobu desu	It's OK/ all right
suki desu (suki pronounced ski)	I like it
suki dewa arimasen	I don't like it

West meets East: hints on traditions and attitudes in the Land of the Rising Sun

Education
An obsession

It might seem curious to begin a section such as this with a discussion of education, but, whether consciously or not, education has become a Japanese obsession.

After the Second World War many inequalities in Japanese society were evened out by the reforms which abolished titles and broke up the huge landed estates, and since this time there has been a far more even distribution of income in society than exists in the US or western Europe. Status is very often derived from one's work (especially in urban areas) and entry to the most prestigious areas of government service and to the top private companies is the preserve of graduates from the nation's leading universities. Ambitious parents must think of their child's education early on.

An educated society

Every child goes to school in Japan and literacy rates are the highest in the world. About 90 per cent of children go on to senior high school after six years of compulsory elementary education and three years in a junior high school. More than a third of Japanese teenagers go to university or a similar institution. Japan's impressive educational record has been a leading factor in its economic success. (Impressive in that so many people have received a higher education, though the Japanese are very conscious that they have produced very few Nobel Prize winners.) The country has highly educated workers not only at the top, but at every level of business and industry. A shop assistant or a lift girl are both likely to be well-read and educated.

The pressures that education puts on a Japanese family are immense. At every stage of school life a Japanese child has to take examinations, and success in these determines the nature of the next stage. The whole process of exam taking is known as 'the examination hell'. The mother has the greatest responsibility for the children's education, because she is at home and for most of the time the father is not. The 'education momma' (*kyoiku mama*) who devotes her life totally to supervising her children's education is an important feature of postwar Japan. There is also the *stage momma* who devotes herself to 'developing' the artistic or sporting talents of her children.

'The examination hell'

Generally speaking a Japanese child receives coaching outside school as well as in school, often in *juku* – private schools which prepare children for particular exams, or which give coaching in music, ballet, baseball and other skills. A Japanese child regularly has a lot of homework and the household often revolves around children's homework and trips to and from private lessons.

For a long time many Japanese have wondered whether these pressures are not rather too much. The recent outbreak of violence at junior high schools has made a peaceful, law-abiding society very worried. Teachers question whether it is their role to prepare pupils for exams for so much of school time. Some subjects clearly do not benefit from the system. The most important of these is language learning. Children are prepared for exams in translation, but not to be speakers of English. There is much criticism, too, of university life, which seems slack and aimless after the rigours and discipline of school. But quite how to change the educational system in a highly competitive education-conscious society no one knows; and many conclude that it is the hard work of school years which ingrain the Japanese character and make it what it is. (In school Japanese children are emphatically taught the significance and importance of harmony and team work.)

Problems without a solution?

Women
Where are the
feminists?

Japan may seem something of a problem for western feminists, because although Japanese women hold very few important positions in government, business and industry (for example, of 8,227 senior civil servants 42 are women), they seem to be doing little to change things. There have been no demands as in the West to make a reality of the constitution under which women are guaranteed equality at work (the constitution of 1946 was drawn up under American guidance).

But it is useful to bear in mind three things. First, that Japanese women are slowly breaking through into spheres of life once exclusive to men. Second, the attitudes of young people are markedly different from those of elders and they do not see male and female roles so rigidly defined in society. Third, it must be admitted, the prime aim of Japanese women is to get married and have a family. Indeed, many Japanese women argue that they are more fortunate than men. They stay at home and do not have to spend an exhausting day at work. They have control of the family's finances (a tradition in Japan, facilitated by the bank transfer system) and of the home. With the modernization of the Japanese home they have the leisure to take up sports and classes and become involved in other social activities which their husbands have little time for.

Working for a
foreign company

The material well-being and happiness of so many women should not obscure the fact that many girls who would like a career are frustrated. The *average* Japanese company likes to employ women until their late twenties (at the latest) by which time they expect them to have got married and to have their own home. Young women at work are thought of as clerical helpers, receptionists and tea-makers and not as people following a career. In the face of this many Japanese women see their salvation in working for a foreign company which has an office in Japan. The foreign company gives them the opportunity to earn higher salaries, the chance of real promotion and perhaps the opportunity to work abroad.

As in so many areas of Japanese life, there is

inevitably a tension between traditional practices – in this case keeping women out of the higher echelons of administration – and the changed mood and expectations of the new generation.

The family is the core of Japanese society. A Japanese man places his family name on the gate or on his front door, and the home is a private and revered place. The Japanese have not adjusted to the idea of people living away from home, apart from students and husbands working temporarily in another place. It is usual for children to stay at home until they are married (though boys as well as girls receive training at school in cookery and home crafts), and there is the feeling that old people should not live alone but should be incorporated into the family.

This perhaps is the most difficult point for the modern family. At one time it was taken as a matter of course that the eldest son both inherited the family property and looked after his parents in their old age. Now many houses are too small to accommodate an aged parent, and many daughters-in-law are unwilling to take on the traditional responsibility. For the first time people are beginning to speak of loneliness in Japanese society, as the old family system breaks down and the smaller family unit emerges.

The elderly

One third of marriages in Japan are arranged marriages or *o miai*, and many Japanese couples, if not dependent on anything so formal as an arrangement have required 'well-meaning' third parties to bring them together. There are (inevitably) some western misconceptions about arranged marriages. They do not represent forced marriages. Rather there is an attempt by family, family friends or employers to put people from compatible backgrounds in touch with each other. Courtship is a much more restrained affair (kissing in public shocks most Japanese). A lot of young Japanese want to travel abroad to experience the freedom and opportunities that young Americans and Europeans have, or which the young Japanese believe that they have.

Marriage
O miai and true love

The marriage ceremony and finding a home

The marriage ceremony in Japan is incredibly elaborate (and expensive) and is the occasion when not just two people, but two families, are brought together. The newly-weds used to go to live with the husband's family, and the wife was ruled by her mother-in-law. To say the very least this pattern is fast disappearing and it is more likely for one or both families to give financial support to the young couple in the expensive business of finding somewhere to live. (The Japanese have coined a new saying to express what young women want from a marriage: 'ie-tsuki, kah-tsuki, baba-nuki' – 'a house, a car but no mother-in-law'.)

Children
An honoured place

Children are greatly honoured in Japan and the Japanese are sometimes shocked at the casual way in which westerners treat their children. It is very unusual, for example, for the Japanese to have babysitters to look after their children while they go out for the night. When a Japanese family goes out to dine in a restaurant, it is often the children who are put in the place of honour. Two of the major festivals in Japan are Girls' Day (3 March) and Boys' or Children's Day (5 May).

Jizō

You may see the rather sad sights of *jizō* as you travel around Japan. These are (usually) carved stone statues of the Buddhist guardian deity of children. The statue might be draped with a red cloth hood or bib. You may perhaps see a jizō at a roadside with a bunch of flowers placed at the base. This probably commemorates a child who has died in a road accident (at that very spot). At Kamakura there is a huge temple set aside for jizō, the statues representing aborted babies. Abortion is easy in Japan and has no stigma attached to it.

Pleasures and pains

Most babies and small children sleep with their parents, in the same bed or on the same futon, and because of the alarm caused by children's behaviour in recent years children who have separate bedrooms now frequently have the door removed. The concept of a Japanese home is that it is a place without barriers, both physically and psychologically. To many westerners Japanese children are over-indulged and it may be that, consciously or not, Japanese parents seek to compensate for the rigours of school and work life which lie ahead.

Divorce, though easy, carries a strong social stigma and huge financial disadvantages.

Divorce

The Japanese are covered by comprehensive state medical insurance, though they often prefer to buy drugs at a pharmacy for small ailments (much more can be bought without a prescription than, for example, in Britain) and many pay for private treatment from doctors. Doctors and dentists are the wealthiest professional group in Japanese society, but medical training is extremely expensive and it might be some years before a doctor or dentist has been reimbursed for the costs of his tuition.

Health
Insurance

The traditional Japanese diet is generally considered healthy. It is low in cholesterol and extremely nutritious. However, it is rather high in salt. As the nation's diet has changed with the introduction of more meat and bread since the War the Japanese are experiencing a rise in obesity and heart disease. Yet the people of the country are avid keep-fitters, and many companies and factories open the day with organized communal exercise sessions. The Japanese have the highest life expectancy of any race in the world.

Diet

Perhaps the biggest divide between generations in Japan is over the concept of leisure. Simply put, the younger generation are used to the idea of leisure and want time to play sports, go shopping and travel. But older Japanese men were brought up to believe that work should fill life, with perhaps occasional traditional holidays. Most businessmen still receive two weeks' vacation a year, and many are in the habit of surrendering this time and staying at work. Some older employees, now presented with a two-day weekend, are at a loss to know what to do with so much free time. At the same time they may be

Leisure
Changing concepts

shocked at some younger members of their organization refusing to do overtime and going home punctually.

Home life It must be remembered that the concept of home life as conceived by westerners, where activities like gardening and home maintenance play a prominent part, hardly exists in Japan (the Japanese think gardening is for the elderly). Home for working men is perhaps only a place in which to sleep. Japanese social life is interlinked with work life. Home is cramped – the office is spacious. At work there is a good canteen and after work employees go out to drink or eat together. 'Dropping out' is almost inconceivable in Japan, because it would be like dropping out of life itself.

Retirement
Lifetime
employment

Retirement, as you can imagine, poses great psychological problems for the Japanese worker, but there are financial difficulties too. Lifetime employment is not universal and, very generally speaking, applies in larger companies and not small. Roughly half of the work force retires between the ages of 55 and 60 and then seeks part-time employment until 60 or beyond (pensions are payable at the age of 60 or 65). The size of a pension depends on a person's contribution to company pension schemes and to private savings (20 per cent of income in Japan is saved – one of the highest rates in the world) for support in old age and to pay for responsibilities such as education.

An ageing
society

The birth-rate has steadily declined since the war while life expectancy has risen sharply (for men the average life expectancy is 74 and for women, 79). At present 9 per cent of the population is over 65, but by the turn of the century that figure will be 16 per cent (and by 2020 over 21 per cent). There will be a decreasingly smaller workforce to provide the greater social benefits needed. That is why many Japanese now speak of the crisis of the ageing society, and the topic is daily a matter of earnest discussion in the media.

We have already gathered that it would be unthinkable in Japan not to want to work. The *meishi* (name card) which a company employee has gives his name, employer and position in the company. Sometimes professionals and the self-employed list their home address too. It is studied very carefully by anyone it is presented to. The (rare) sons of the wealthy who do not work are called '*dōraku-musoku*' (wasters). So far Japan has been very fortunate in keeping its unemployment figures low (about 3 per cent). Japan's economy has expanded steadily throughout the twentieth century to take on new workers, and service industries are labour intensive.

Work
The need to work

There is a strict hierarchy at work, and promotion for many positions is dependent on seniority. Promoting a whiz kid is not popular with the Japanese, who tend to believe that the aggravation caused would not make the promotion worthwhile. Most company presidents are aged, as indeed are Japan's leading politicians. (Former Prime Minister Tanaka was a notable exception.)

Promotion

Work confers dignity in Japan, and the Japanese are ready to explain that unremitting hard work has been essential throughout Japanese history and that only now, for the first time, is there a whole generation of *nouveaux riches*. The Japanese are conscious of their country's limited space and natural resources (90 per cent of the raw materials its industry requires are imported) and there is not one Japanese who thinks that the country's prosperity and power are something to be taken for granted.

A sense of insecurity

The idea of the group is extremely important in Japan. In western societies a person has particular workmates and friends, but in Japan the sense of a group involves something more than this. The group takes precedence over the individual, which is rarely the case in the West. For whereas (in simple terms) individualism is seen (at its best) in the West as a person's endeavours to do what their conscience tells them, in Japan it is much more readily equated with egotism and selfishness.

What makes Japan tick: the group
The group versus the individual

Outward and inward feelings   The Japanese also use the concepts of *tatemae* and *honne*. Tatemae is often translated as truthfulness and honne as true mind. It is possibly easier for the westerner to grasp these ideas if they are likened to our sense of the distinction between inner and outer feelings. Tatemae is the rule which is unanimously accepted by the whole group and honne is one individual's point of view. If the two differ, the Japanese see no ambiguity in a situation.

The making of a group   However, it should not be forgotten that for a group to be effective in Japan, it must reflect every change of feeling and mood of its members. The work group takes a long time to reach any decision and has to engage in lengthy debate and consultation. Yet its unanimity on a particular issue means that the execution of its decision is effective and fast.

There are other strong bonds and groups in Japan, in particular those originating in school and university, and alumni are a powerful force in Japan. At work many graduates of the same school or university stick together. The *sempai – kohai* relationship in the work world (senior and junior) by which an older person helps and teaches a younger man and in return receives his unswerving loyalty, often rests on the foundation of a shared educational background.

Place, especially a village location, may give rise to strong group feeling, and indeed, it is Japan's predominantly rural past (until the Meiji period the country was mainly rural) which is thought to lie at the origins of groupism. Co-operation was essential for agricultural communities to survive, and a Japanese saying runs: 'in times of fire and flood, who could stand alone?'

One feature of groupism which works very much to society's advantage is the fact that groupism is not the equivalent of exclusivity. Groups expand readily to take in newcomers. The Japanese group is perhaps not the English club or the American fraternity; it is malleable and flexible, working according to unseen rules.

Harmony   Groupism reflects the Japanese love for harmony, for the Japanese logically ask what good disharmony can do. The Japanese feel bound to their group, but they also feel obliged to maintain good relations with neighbours. Ideally they believe there should be a general 'sweetness' in society. Litigation in civil matters is rare in Japanese life and is interpreted as a sign that the Japanese way has broken down; often, a judge will ask plaintiffs to go away and reconsider before coming to him for a judgement.

Obligation
A rosy picture

Perhaps for some this paints all too rosy a picture. On a train an old lady is ignored and not offered a seat, while elsewhere others are in distress and passers-by feign indifference. One example of the kind of situation that often annoys foreign visitors is, say when a drunk harangues a foreigner and no one comes to the rescue – which they do not! We have now entered the realm of obligation, and though the Japanese will strive not to conflict with others, they feel they cannot be obligated to everyone. Every individual already feels the burden of family and group loyalties (there are also, of course, the strengths which these loyalties bring). To the outside world they must be somewhat aloof. If someone helps a person who is in distress, this sets up an obligation on the other person's part which possibly neither party will want.

Balance

The Japanese are ingrained with a sense of balance. Favours must be returned. Twice a year there are the somewhat exploitative occasions of *go-seibo* (December) and *o-chūgen* (summer) when people give gifts to pay debts of gratitude. If one makes a prayer at a shrine or temple, one must make a small offering: one cannot ask for something without giving in return.

Revenge

Much is perhaps made of the concept of revenge because people have seen samurai movies on TV. However, there does not seem to be a more sinister reverse side to the strong sense of indebtedness that prevails. It is doubtful, nevertheless, that a person would be forgiven for seriously and deliberately harming a Japanese.

Society and the individual Japanese society is secure and tightly knit, yet it cannot give the individual the degree of independence that many westerners have. But the use to which westerners put this freedom often leaves the Japanese puzzled – we seem to have a poor and limited home life and to suffer a large degree of social and political disharmony.

Religion
Eclecticism The average Japanese is highly eclectic in the matter of religion. In Japan there are 98 million followers of Shinto, 88 million Buddhists and under 1 million Christians. The population of Japan is approximately 120 millions! The average Japanese man or women now claims not to have a religion, but at birth, marriage and death and at special times in the year, particularly New Year and O Bon (when ancestors are remembered) people follow Japan's great traditional ceremonies.

Death Funerals are elaborate and expensive (they are invariably Buddhist) and the plot where the family mausoleum is located may, if it is auspiciously sited, be worth more than any of the family's possessions, including their home. It is customary for mourners to give the family of the deceased a small sum of money called *koden* (now given to help the family at a difficult time). Mourners pour a little salt over themselves for purification before they go home. Cremation and not burial is customary.

Being a good Japanese citizen Whether to take the Japanese claim seriously (a claim particularly strong among the young) that they are not a religious people is difficult to say. The damage caused to the country by the Second World War was quickly repaired and Japan soon flourished again. But the faith of a generation which had believed in the divinity of the emperor and the divine mission of Japan was shattered.

Most Japanese people are not guided by formal religious tenets as the West might believe, but they do want to be thought of as good Japanese citizens. Precisely what this entails is difficult to estimate – but the Japanese generally believe in and practise kind-

ness, honesty and hard work, and that is surely a solid
foundation for any society.

The discussion of suicide in Japan has assumed far
greater dimensions in the West than the reality
warrants, for Japan by no means heads the suicide
tables. What perhaps fascinates the westerner is the
concept of death as a means of preserving honour,
and as recently as 1945 tens of thousands of Japanese
soldiers and civilians committed suicide rather than
fall into the hands of the Allies.

Suicide
Western ideas

The way of the samurai was *bushido*, a code of loyalty
and honour similar to the chivalric code of medieval
Europe. In a dishonourable situation there was no
way out but *seppuku* or *harakiri*, which required the
samurai to commit suicide by stabbing himself in the
stomach (believed to be the true repository of all
feeling). It is true that suicides in Japan still tend to
occur over matters of shame – accumulating debts or
disgrace at work, and even today a member of a work
group might commit suicide to exonerate his group
(upon which the company gives his family some cash
payment (*koden*); however, if he resigns there is
nothing). But the Japanese were, for example, pro-
foundly shocked at the last known example of
seppuku, that of the celebrated writer Yukio Mishima
in 1970 (a friend beheaded him after the ceremony).
The sense of shame and disgrace is strong in Japan,
but suicides are part of the same sad stories in human
life as they are elsewhere, and the West should not
look for knightly ideals which have passed away.

Bushido

The emperor is a shy, frail figure, now 84, living in
moated seclusion in the Imperial palace in Tokyo.
Every year Emperor Hirohito symbolically plants
rice in the palace grounds, a duty he performs as
Shinto's highest ranking priest. At one time his figure
was hedged with divinity, but this ended in 1947
when the new constitution proclaimed him 'the
symbol of the state and unity of the people'. In 1945 it
was Hirohito's intervention which ended fighting.
His plea to the Japanese people to bear the unbearable

The emperor
*Personality
and power*

and surrender brought hostilities to an immediate end.

The future
For many Japanese the emperor (194th in unbroken succession to the throne) is a symbol of Japan's history and the purity of the Japanese race. (It would, for example, be unthinkable for a member of the Imperial family to marry a foreign prince or princess.) But the 'remoteness' of the Imperial family is a serious problem in the TV age. Though the empress might sit an American child on her lap in Disneyland on the Imperial visit to the United States, such a spontaneous gesture could not happen in Japan. Not only is there tradition to contend with, but the problems of security are immense. The present emperor's position is assured and unique, but of the future of the Imperial system one cannot be so sure.

National attitudes
Homogeneity
Japanese society is one of the most homogeneous in the world, and for such a large nation with such an important position in the world, it is remarkably so. There is one large ethnic minority in Japan, some 669,800 Koreans, and though there are occasional difficulties between the Japanese and the Japanese-Korean community, they cause no more than ripples on the smooth surface of Japanese society.

A part of or apart from Asia?
The Japanese think of themselves first and foremost as Japanese. The differences between Japanese society and all others are readily apparent (and if anything are emphasized by any book or article on Japan). The Japanese do not deny that Japan is Asian, but they do not seem as aware of their Asian neighbours as their geographical position would suggest. Not only is there the isolation factor (Japan was totally isolated during the Edo period), but since Meiji, Japan has learnt from, competed with and measured herself against the West. Many psychologists have pointed to the fact that there is a light skin preference among the Japanese – and this would militate against any change in Japan's westward stance.

The Japanese are one of the few peoples in Asia who did not know westerners as colonizers. Westerners were always businessmen, missionaries and teachers, and it is as teachers (in the broadest sense) that they are often seen. (This is why perhaps the Japanese cannot see themselves as teachers – of technology, industrial organization, etc. – to the West.) Westerners in Japan are respected and generally treated very kindly – their complaint is usually that they are unable to become as Japanese as they would like!

Japan and the West

Japan tends to be regarded by the US as a bastion of democracy and capitalism in a crucial but uncertain part of the world. Ironically Japan, once defeated and disarmed by America, is now being encouraged by her in the strongest terms to play a bigger role in her own protection and in giving a lead to the nations of the region. The Japanese people were understandably revolted by militarism, and the atomic holocaust of 1945 has left indelible scars. Governments have to redefine Japan's international role cautiously – but there is no doubt that this is being done. Japan's economic success makes it inevitable that Japan must play a more active role in Asian and world affairs generally. Japan's defence budget in recent years has grown at a greater pace than almost any other area of government spending.

Japan's international position
The US-Japan connection

There can be no relaxation in relations with Russia while Russia possesses the Northern Islands. The islands are heavily militarized and the Soviet strike capacity against Japan is immense.

Relations with China have changed considerably in recent years. In 1972 normal diplomatic relations were restored between the two countries following the abrupt decision of the Nixon administration to put Sino-American relations on a better footing. America's negotiations with China had been kept secret from their Japanese allies, and when the new policy was announced it caused great offence to the Japanese. However, Japan has benefited enormously from the diplomatic changes. Taiwan has been in no position to retaliate against Japan or America for their

Attitudes to Russia and China

normalization of relations with communist China, so that Japan's profitable trade with Taiwan has continued, while the changed diplomatic climate has also enabled Japan to increase trade with China.

Careful handling of neighbours Japan treads carefully in Asia, trying not, with its great wealth and power, to appear a conqueror in a new guise. Prime Minister Nakasone in a bid to be humble walks down the edge of welcoming red carpets on visits to neighbouring countries. This seems to symbolize Japan's approach to her neighbours in Asia.

Japan is a great Pacific power. It is the major or second trading partner of every region in the area. Japan is Australia's largest customer, buying iron ore, coal, wool and meat. Many young Japanese now contemplate surfing holidays in Australia as well as the more conventional trips to California, London and Paris. (The Japanese also visit Taiwan, Korea and other places in South-East Asia in large numbers.)

There's no place like home There are still comparatively few Japanese living abroad; there are descendants of Japanese in large numbers in Hawaii, California and Brazil alone. Japanese businessmen abroad are coached in the ways of their host country, but Japanese communities remain tightly knit and inward-looking (with Japanese parents even more worried than usual about their children's education). The communities contain model citizens: polite, law-abiding and honest, and the investment their presence represents generally has been keenly sought by their host countries. Japanese culture, the Japanese way, remains locked in Japan – but perhaps it can only flourish on the islands of Japan themselves.

Doing business with the Japanese

Western manufacturers have many gripes about Japan, but what do the Japanese have to say in answer to these?

Japanese markets are open: there are quotas on only 27 foreign products; tariffs average 3.5 per cent (figures below the US and Europe).

There is no discrimination against the foreign importer: everyone has to deal with the same procedures at customs and with the same internal distribution system.

Many Japanese consumers prefer foreign goods for snobbish reasons, especially food and fashion.

Time: foreign companies treat Japan as a far-eastern outpost; visits by foreign businessmen are short and invariably part of a long tour: foreigners posted to Japan do not stay long enough; foreign companies do far too little market research on the country and often try to sell wholly unsuitable goods.

The Japanese will warm to anyone who has some knowledge of Japan. They feel that as a nation they are not understood and are sometimes deliberately misunderstood. The Japanese think less in terms of particular deals and more in terms of establishing long-term relationships. Contracts are seen as a basis for action rather than the parameters of a transaction. The Japanese rarely go to court and consequently there are fewer lawyers in Japan than in the city of Washington.

Following from the above, the Japanese will not be rushed into making decisions, and will not do business with people they do not trust. Persistence pays: keeping in touch, making visits, nurturing the market.

General points

Getting help   The Japan External Trade Relations Organization (JETRO) describes itself as a 'non profit-making organization for the promotion of trade between Japan and other countries. JETRO's activities are mainly supported by subsidies from the Japanese Government. Current activities include market research, data dissemination, import and export promotion, public relations, and trade fairs.'

The fact that JETRO is a Japanese government agency means that the pursuit of Japanese interests must be its *raison d'être*. JETRO tends to co-operate with the information services of a particular country, for example, those of the Department of Trade and Industry in the UK. It has 78 offices in 59 countries:

Headquarters   2–5, Toranomon 2-Chome
               Minato-Ku
               Tokyo 105
               (tel. 582–5511)

UK office   Japan Trade Centre
               19/25 Baker Street
               London WIM 1AE
               (tel. 01–486–6761)

US office   Japan Trade Center, New York
               44th Floor, McGraw Hill Building
               1221 Avenue of the Americas
               New York, N.Y. 10020–1060
               (tel. (212) 997–0400)

There are also JETRO centres in Chicago, Houston, Los Angeles and San Francisco. In Britain the main office is supported by a number of subsidiary JETRO offices (dealing with shipping, export insurance and metal).

British businessmen and women are very fortunate in being able to consult an excellent body of advisers:

Exports to Japan Unit
   British Overseas Trade Board
   Department of Trade and Industry
   1, Victoria Street
   London SW1H 0ET
   (tel. 01–215–3842)

A booklet available from the unit, *Hints to Exporters to Japan*, offers an excellent introduction to the Japanese market. (Other material and reading lists are also available.)

Another obvious source of advice and information for the British business executive would be the Commercial Department of the British Embassy in Tokyo (265–5511), or the British Consulate-General in Osaka (231–3355). Other places to contact are:

British Chamber of Commerce in Japan
    PO Box 2145,
    World Import Mart Branch
    Toshima-ku
    Tokyo 107
    (tel. 987–1620)

The Kansai Committee
    c/o Price Waterhouse Co.
    Osaka Centre Building
    68–3 Kita Kyutaro-machi, 4-chome
    Higashi-Ku Osaka
    (tel. 252–6791)

American personnel can seek information and advice from:

The Trade Department
    The American Embassy
    10–1 Akasaka
    1-Chome
    Tokyo
    (tel. 583–7141)

The American Chamber of Commerce
    7th Floor, Fukide Building No.2
    1–21, Toranomon
    4-Chome
    Minato-ku
    Tokyo
    (tel. 433–5381)

Japanese companies

Japan is a land of private enterprise (plus ministerial guidance) where a company looms large. To work for a good company seems to be the ambition of all young people. Business is an honourable way of life

which, it has been claimed, has managed to combine
the samurai spirit – bushido – with the spirit of
modern capitalism. Certainly, work of this kind is not
just a job. One commits oneself for life (or, say, until
the age of 57 to 60), and gives complete loyalty to the
company. It is a mystery to many Japanese how and
why westerners change their jobs so often, answering
adverts, uprooting themselves and transferring loyalties.

*Big versus
small*
The companies which are most famous outside Japan
are the *sogo shosha* or trading companies. These are
groups which combine banking, manufacturing and
retailing. Nine sogo shosha control over half Japan's
import-export business. Six large groups control over
one third of the Japanese economy (Mitsubishi,
Mitsui and Sumimoto, and the big banks Fuji, Daiichi
Kangyo and Sanwa).

If a foreign businessman is dealing with a large
company, he will encounter expertise and sophisti-
cation to a high degree, and doubtless he will deal
with people who have travelled widely abroad or may
have been stationed overseas. Generally, in Japan the
smaller the company the less prestige it has. In a small
company you might well encounter Japanese people
who have not met foreigners before, and here you
need to be more careful of Japanese susceptibilities.
However, in selecting a company to do business with,
a small company may well be better than a big one.
For whereas a large company may swallow up your
business and assume that the name alone will sell the
goods, a smaller company will have more time to pay
attention to your particular needs.

Organization
At the top of a Japanese company is the board,
comprising chairman, president, vice-president and
other directors. There are one to three vice-presidents
in a Japanese company and these are powerful figures.

The chief of a division is called a *bucho*. He reports
to the board of directors and in some cases may also
be a member of the board himself. He administers his
division, giving orders to the chief of each section, the
kacho. The kacho is a vitally important figure in the

Japanese company. At his level all routine business is dispatched without reference above. A man may become a kacho at about the age of forty, and it may well be that he does not rise above this point.

The sense of hierarchy in a Japanese company is very strong. Often gradations of salary are not great, but enormous respect is given to the position a person holds. (The Japanese are able at a glance to weigh up the personnel of a department as the seating-plan rigidly reflects position.)

Hierarchy and democracy

For all the sense of hierarchy, Japanese companies are also noted for their 'democracy'. The *ringisho*, a paper outlining a company's proposals, goes the round of the offices and everyone concerned with the proposal is expected to read it and append his seal in turn according to rank. Cynically, one might say that reading the ringisho is merely rubber-stamping the company's decision, but to be seen to have employees behind a plan is vital for the Japanese company, and if there were dissent, one wonders whether a project would go ahead. The fact that so many people have to be involved before a decision is made in Japan makes decision-making a slow business.

As suggested, negotiations in Japan may well take longer than in other countries. These will be lengthened by elaborate entertaining. A foreign businessman may well have travelled a long way, and a free day before the round starts might be a good idea. All this adds up to making a trip to Japan longer than might be the case for another country.

Your first trip to Japan: hints and advice

Never simply turn up in Japan. Give Japanese companies ample notice of your visit and some idea of what you wish to discuss. It may also be a good idea to notify embassies, cultural bodies and ministries in advance.

Businessmen should not take wives along on a trip unless they are prepared to be very independent. The Japanese rarely take their wives with them on business, and are surprised when foreigners do. Entertainment in Japan will be without wives present, and it is doubtful you will be entertained at home. If

your wife does come with you, your hosts will feel
obliged to look after her, perhaps to the extent of
providing a guide and interpreter. This is a service
businessmen and wives may hesitate to accept.

Foreign businesswomen are accepted, since the
Japanese understand that women play a powerful role
in the industrial world of other countries, though
they barely figure in the upper ranks of their own. A
foreign businesswoman will therefore be treated with
great courtesy, but entertainment will probably be
confined to restaurants and not include bars or night
clubs.

Dress formally – men, a dark suit and white shirt,
women a suit or dress, somewhat conservative
perhaps!

It is well known that Japan is a land of present
giving. The visitor should take gifts for his hosts and a
few small extras in case. Gifts representing your
company or your home country are particularly
special to the Japanese.

Be loyal to your company throughout your deal-
ings in Japan, even if you are on the brink of moving
on. Disloyalty is looked upon with feudal horror.

You should have a good stock of name cards
(*meishi*). These can be printed in Japan if necessary.
Ideally, a name card should be in English on one side
and in Japanese on the other. It should also be fairly
large and the writing distinct. (The Japanese sometimes wonder at foreign visitors' small name cards!)
Try and be accurate on your card about your
position. Rank is vitally important in Japan. If the
Japanese find they have been entertaining a junior as a
senior executive, this could mean the end of a
promising friendship. The Japanese present and
receive meishi with great ceremony. You cannot hope
to emulate this, but you should offer and receive
meishi slowly and with some care. On no account just
pocket someone's card. For example, if you are sitting
at a meeting keep the card out on the table. This
shows respect (and helps you to remember the
person's name).

Let the Japanese decide whether first names should,
if ever, be used. The Japanese often use a person's title

in address, for example, Tanaka Shacho.

Westerners can look a little odd bowing to the Japanese and tend to feel awkward. A slight inclination of the head comes naturally after some time, and that is probably sufficient for a foreign visitor to appear polite to the Japanese in all situations. Prepare, however, to have your hand shaken frequently, as the Japanese think this is the western way.

The Japanese are most hospitable and will surely entertain you well. If you are asked what you want to eat, plump for something Japanese. (The Japanese often have Chinese food for a banquet or top celebration.) Don't try to talk business during a meal unless it is your only chance of doing so. The Japanese strictly compartmentalize business and pleasure.

Controversial issues are not good subjects for informal conversation. On the other hand if a Japanese person insists on discussing a topic you wish to avoid, you might say something such as 'No one talks about that in my country.' Never visibly get angry or shout; this will show people present you are weak and ill-disciplined.

You may be called on to make speeches without prior warning, since with English as a first language giving a speech is considered easy.

Have sympathy for the Japanese who are trying to speak to you in English. Playing host to a foreign visitor probably entails enormous hard work and concentration. Quickly assess your host's language ability and try to adjust your vocabulary and use of idioms and slang accordingly.

At a meeting check periodically that everyone has understood what you are saying. If necessary, give a resumeè of what you have covered. If you can offer Japanese participants something to read as well as listen to, that will be appreciated.

Pay particular attention to numbers. High figures may cause confusion even to the excellent English speaker. Remember that most Japanese are more familiar with American than British English, so take care for example with billions, floor numbers, etc.

The Japanese value the saying 'Silence is golden.'

Do not attempt to fill every gap in the conversation. Silences are useful for both sides to reflect, and you may, in your haste to speak, make unnecessary concessions in bargaining.

Do not assume that someone not speaking English does not understand it. Be careful to include everyone in the group in the conversation. Do not give all your attention to the most competent English speaker – he may well be young and of low rank in the company. (Moreover, because he is so good at English, he may even be regarded with slight suspicion by his colleagues!)

Take care with yes and no (see p.131).

When a Japanese hears the phrase *Kangaete okimasu* (I'll think it over) he assumes there is no hope for a proposal and that a person is saying no. Rather than say 'I'll think about it', it is better to be specific and say, for example, 'I have to speak to my company in London about this.'

It is not the Japanese habit to write letters to the other side in a business deal summarizing the progress and results of a meeting. You may of course do so, but such a letter, which might almost be contractual in some parts of the world, is just a letter in Japan.

Letters of thanks are considered courteous. When the Japanese write in English they conventionally end their letters by telling people to take good care of their health. You might reciprocate in your reply. A lot of Japanese companies employ a native speaker whose job it is to check the English in letters and help generally with interpretation.

Settling in: some useful organizations

British Council	Tokyo (235–8031), Kyoto (075–791–7151). Good libraries – books may be borrowed (Alien Registration Card required and payment of ¥3,000 per year). Kenkyusha Eigo Centre (269–4331). Same building as British Council, Tokyo – courses in Japanese language and culture. British council publication: *British Studies. A List of Societies in Japan*.	**Libraries and cultural centres**
Tokyo American Center	Library streamlined, up-to-date, for reference only (436–0901).	
American Club	Plush, expensive, all facilities, including library with video collection (538–8381).	
Australia–Japan Academic and Cultural Centre	Small, friendly, books on Australia, occasional lectures – a second home for Australians (498–4143).	
International House	Many facilities, reasonably priced accommodation for members, good library overlooking a superb Japanese garden (470–4611).	
Asiatic Society of Japan	Good library, monthly talks on learned themes (586–1548).	
Japan Foundation Library	Internationally famous collections for scholars and the high-minded (263–4491).	
Diet Library	By far the largest library in Japan. One third of its 4	

million volumes are in English (581–2331).

Foreign Correspondents' Club — For the latest updates and gossip, but membership is restricted to those holding a press card, etc. (211–3161).

National groupings The following national societies offer a range of activities and go out of their way to welcome new arrivals to the country.

Japan-British Society (211–8027). Contact this society for information on the St George's Society and the St Andrew's Society.
Canada-Japan Society (581–0925)
Australia-Japan Society (281–9372)
Japan-New Zealand Society (through the New Zealand Embassy, (467–2271)).

Churches A full list is carried in the Saturday edition of the *Japan Times* with times of services etc.

Business associations
British Chamber of Commerce	(987–1620)
American Chamber of Commerce	(433–5381)
Canadian Chamber of Commerce	(414–7111)
Australian Chamber of Commerce	(501–7031)

Teachers' association The Japanese Association of Language Teachers or JALT (075–221–2251) has branches throughout Japan and runs many activities. At the annual conference in the autumn there is a major book fair, speeches, workshops and much talk and rumours about jobs going.

Learning Japanese There are plenty of schools which specialize in teaching Japanese to foreigners. The YMCA, for example, have modestly priced courses. Ask for one or two trial lessons if you are not sure what a school has to offer. Learning Japanese at home without lessons rarely works.

Clearly *Coping with Japan* is just a start. You can now begin to unravel Japan at your own pace and in your own way. Every joy and *sayonara*!

Suggestions for further reading

Edwin O. Reischauer is a noted Japanologist. His book *The Japanese* (Tuttle, 1978) is a superb introduction to the country. His *Japan, the Story of a Nation* (Tuttle, 1980) gives an excellent account of the country's historical development.

Chie Nakane's *Japanese Society* (Penguin, 1973) is an interesting study of Japanese society, particularly fascinating in its discussion of the formation and structure of the group, and the relations of the individual to society.

Discover Japan is now published as a paperback (2 vols) by Kodansha International Ltd (first edn 1982). It was previously published in 1975 as *A Hundred Things Japanese* and *A Hundred More Things Japanese*. The books each contain a large collection of essays written by a number of different authors and are illustrated throughout. The topics covered vary from mushrooms to *meishi*, and from foreigners to *futon*.

Nippon, the Land and its People, first published by the New Japan Steel Company in 1978, is an excellent guide to the country.

A Cultural Dictionary of Japan, ed. Momoo Yamaguchi and Setsuko Kojima (The Japan Times Ltd, 1979), makes an indispensable reference book.

The Encyclopaedia of Japan (Kodansha, 1983) is also a superb reference work, written in clear English and with suggestions for further reading at the ends of most entries.

The Japan Travel Manual (issued every year by the Japan National Tourist Organization) is also worth noting. It is an excellent publication containing the latest information on accommodation and travel. Free copies are available at many travel agencies and from other organizations promoting travel to Japan.

Language   The Berlitz *Japanese for Travellers* (published and written by the staff of Editions Berlitz, a division of MacMillan S.A., 1974) is a handy and useful phrasebook.

Osamu and Nobuko Mitzutani's *An Introduction to Modern Japanese* offers an excellent course in language learning and is accompanied by tapes.

A Guide to Reading and Writing Japanese, ed. Florence Sakade (Tuttle, 1982), is an extremely well-organized book introducing the 1,850 basic *kanji*.

Finally, Jack Seward has written an expert and amusing commentary on the Japanese language, which you should certainly not pass by: *Japanese in action* (Weatherhill, 1981). It is both a useful source for learning words and phrases and a piquant sociological study.

Art   Lawrence Smith and Victor Harris, *Japanese Decorative Arts* (a British Museum publication, 1982) is a readable introduction to the traditional arts of Japan.

Joan Stanley-Baker, *Japanese Art* (Thames and Hudson, 1984) is a very accessible survey of the history of Japanese art with a useful reading list at the end.

Eating out   A very helpful book to pick up on arrival in Japan is Kimiko Nagasawa and Camy Condon's *Eating Cheap in Japan* (Shufunotomo Co., 1982). It is a pocket-size volume which gives a brief description (with pictures) of some 241 foods and drinks.

Touring the country   The very best guide for touring Japan is Ian McQueen's *Japan, a Travel Survival Kit* (Lonely Planet Publications, 1981).

The Japan Travel Bureau publishes a basic guide, *Travel Guide to Japan*.

Junichiro Kuroki and Shinzo Uchida's *Touring Tokyo* (Kodansha, 1979) is a short guide to Tokyo.

A classic marked by beautiful language and invaluable detail is Gouverneur Mosher's *Kyoto, a Contemplative Guide* (Tuttle, 1982).

The businessman or businesswoman might wish to pick up this handy volume on arriving in Japan:

Business

Passport in Japan, published yearly by Business Intercommunications Inc. It gives the latest statistics on the Japanese economy and industry, and contains a large number of useful addresses and telephone numbers. The Mitsubishi Corporation has produced a clear guide to commonly used words in the Japanese business world (and Mitsubishi should know!). It is published by Tokyo-Keizai-Shinpasha, 1984.

Japan Business Obstacles and Opportunities (McKinsey & Co., 1983), does what it says and explains the problems of doing business in Japan. It lists some success stories.

Living in Japan published by the American Chamber of Commerce in Tokyo contains a substantial amount of useful information for the resident.

Settling in Japan

Now You Live in Japan published by the *Japan Times* gives straightforward advice about such problems as housing, banking, taxation (and even dying!) in Japan.

Jean Pearce, a columnist with the *Japan Times*, has had a number of her excellent articles 'Getting Things Done' published under the same title by the *Japan Times*. They were largely written in reply to the queries and concerns of (often frustrated) foreign residents.

Conversion tables

Distance 1 kilometre = 0.62 miles
1 mile = 1.61 km
Roughly:

1 km	⅝ mile
3 km	2 miles
5 km	3 miles
8 km	5 miles
10 km	6 miles

Weight 100 grammes = 3.33 oz; 1 kilometre (1000 g) = 2.2 lb
1 oz = 28.35 g; 1 lb = 0.45 kg
Roughly:

100 g	just under ¼ lb
250 g	½ lb
500 g	1 lb
1 kg	just over 2 lb

Liquid 1 litre (100 centilitres/1000 cubic centimetres) = 1.76
imperial pints/2.11 US pints
1 imp. pint = 0.57 litres; 1 imp. gallon = 4.55 litres
1 US pint = 0.47 litres, 1 US gallon = 3.79 litres
Roughly:

0.5 litres	just under 1 imp. pint/just over 1 US pint
1 litre	just under 2 imp. pints/just over 2 US pints
3.75 litres	1 US gallon
4.5 litres	1 imp. gallon

Length 1 centimetre = 0.39 inches; 1 metre (100 centimetres)
= 39.37 inches/1.094 yards
Roughly:

5 cm	2 inches
1 metre	just over 1 yard

Temperature   °centigrade   °fahrenheit

°centigrade	°fahrenheit
100	212 boiling point
38	100
30	86
25	77
20	68
15	59
10	50
5	41
0	32 freezing point

Japanese script: useful words and signs

directions			
entrance	-iriguchi	入	口
exit	-deguchi	出	口
right	-migi	右	
left	-hidari	左	
north	-kita	北	
south	-minami	南	
east	-higashi	東	
west	-nishi	西	

signs & signals			
emergency exit	-hijōguchi	非常口	
danger	-kiken	危険	
no smoking	-kinen	禁煙	
subway	-chikatetsu	地下鉄	
telephone	-denwa	電話	
hospital	-byōin	病院	

post office 〒

post office	-yūbinkyoku	郵	便 局
stamp	-kitte	切	手
post card	-hagaki	葉	書
envelope	-fūtou	封	筒
express	-sokutatsu	速	達 便
air mail	-kōkūbin	航	空 便
sea mail	-funabin	船	便

necessities!

toilet	-otearai/benjo	お手洗/便所
gentlemen	-danshi·yo	男子用
	(shinshi·yo)	紳士用
ladies	-joshi·yo	女子用
	(fujin·yo)	婦人用

© Hiroshi Umemura 1985

Maps

Regions and major towns of Japan
© Hiroshi Umemura 1985

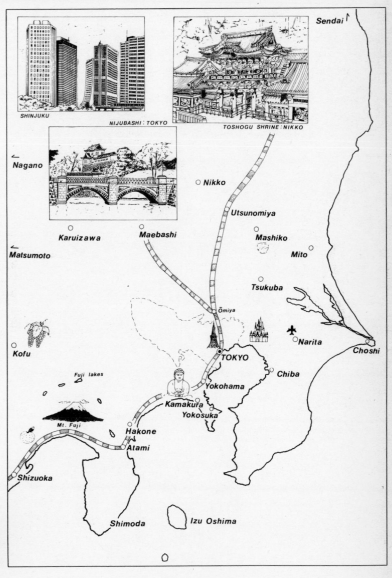

Eastern Japan
© Hiroshi Umemura 1985

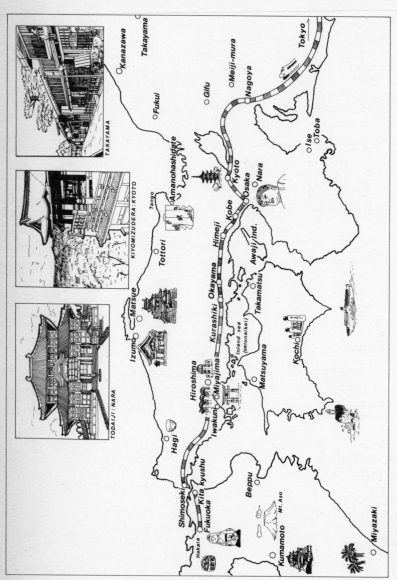

Western Japan
© Hiroshi Umemura 1985

TAKAYAMA

KIYOMIZUDERA : KYOTO

TODAIJI : NARA

Kanazawa
Takayama
Fukui
Gifu
Meiji-mura
Nagoya
Tokyo
Amanohashidate
Tango
Kyoto
Ise
Toba
Tottori
Osaka
Nara
Kobe
Himeji
Matsue
Okayama
Awaji Ind.
Izumo
Kurashiki
Takamatsu
Inland sea
(setonaikai)
Hiroshima
Miyajima
Matsuyama
Iwakuni
Kochi
Hagi
Shimoseki
Kita kyushu
Beppu
Hakata
Fukuoka
Mt. Aso
Kumamoto
Miyazaki

Index

accommodation 7, 11–18
  long stay 15–16
  traditional 11, 12–14
  western 11–12
  see also hotels; *minshuku*; *ryokan*
administrative regions 84–99, 107
age, status given to 132, 139, 142
aikido 75
Ainu people 101
airports 2–3
air travel 2–3
  internal 36
alcohol
  beer 58
  buying 56–7
  and driving, ban on 38
  shō-chū 59
  spirits 58
  ume-shū 59
  whisky 58
  wine 58
  see also sake
Alien Registration Card 9, 28
ambulance service 29
art galleries 62, 89, 95
  see also museums
arts and crafts, traditional 65–8

balance, idea of 145
banks 19, 20–2, 154
bar hostesses 56–8, 74
bars 56–8, 74
baseball 70, 76
bath, Japanese 13, 15, 71–2
bonsai 18, 81
books, buying 64, 86
bowing 16, 131, 157
breakfast 43–4

Buddhism 101–2, 103, 111–12, 116, 146
  see also temples, Buddhist
buses 36–7, 87, 89
  airport 3
bushido (samurai code) 106, 147, 154
business hotels 12

calligraphy (*shodō*) 82, 104
cameras 64, 86
car driving 37
  hire 37, 38
cash, payment in 19–20
ceramics 65–6, 90
cheques, use of 19, 21
cherry blossom 83–4, 118
children
  attitudes to 40, 91, 136–7, 140–1
  registration of 9
  see also education
China, relations with 101–2, 149–50
chopsticks 45
Christianity 97, 106, 111, 146
church services 160
citizenship, idea of 146–7
climate 4, 30–1, 62, 83–4, 97
climbing 94
clothing
  suitable 3–4, 156
  traditional 65
  see also happi coat; *kimono; yukata*
coffee shops (*kissaten*) 43, 55, 56, 86
companies
  Japanese 138, 153–5
  hierarchy in 143, 154–5
  loyalty to 112, 154, 156
  trading companies (*sogo shosha*) 154

Suggestions

This page can be used to send in your suggestions for improving the book. What vital matters have been overlooked? What difficulties and pitfalls have been neglected or glossed over? What else should the intending visitor know about the quirks of the Japanese way of life? Please write and tell us.

If your suggestions are adopted in any future edition, you will receive a free copy in recognition of your services in helping other people cope with Japan.

Please send your suggestions to John Randle, c/o Basil Blackwell Ltd, 108 Cowley Road, Oxford OX4 1JF.

Name ....

Address ....

My suggestions are